Recent Advances in Women Sports

Recent Advances in Women Sports

A Case Study

Yengkhom Santikumar Singh

AKANSHA PUBLISHING HOUSE
NEW DELHI • GUWAHATI • VISAKHAPATNAM

AKANSHA PUBLISHING HOUSE
4649-B/21, Ansari Road
Daryaganj, New Delhi-110002
Phones: 23268193, 09435116718
Email: ektabooks@yahoo.com
visit us: www.akanshapublishinghouse.com

Recent Advances in Women Sports: A Case Study

First Published 2010

ISBN 978-81-8370-246-1

PRINTED IN INDIA

Published by Akansha Publishing House, New Delhi-110002 and printed at Harmain Offset Press, Delhi.

Dedicated
to
(Late) Dr. Ksh. Ratan Singh
And My Parents

Contents

Acknowledgements

Words are inadequate to express thanks to my esteemed guide, Prof. R.N. Dey, Professor, Lakshmibai National University of Physical Education, Gwalior for his valuable direction and supervision, suggestion and guidance at each step in formulation and completion of the study.

I wish to record my sincere gratitude to Major General S.N. Mukherjee, Vice-Chancellor and Prof. L.N. Sarkar, Registrar, Lakshmibai National University of Physical Education, Gwalior for sincere cooperation and help in the formulation and completion of the study.

I acknowledge my special thanks to Prof. S. Mani Singh and Dr. B. Basumatary, Professor and Reader, Lakshmibai National University of Physical Education, Gwalior for suggestion and cooperation from time to time for the successful completion of the study.

I am thankful to all the faculty members and non-teaching staff of Lakshmibai National University of Physical Education, Gwalior for their help in the due course of the study.

I express my affectionate thanks to my father Shri Y. Kunjo Singh, mother Smt. Y. Lalita Devi, only brother Y. Somorjit Singh, Sister Y. Anita Devi and Y. Inaocha Devi and Bichitra Singha who have shared the troubles of my present struggle for education.

I wish to express my never ending heartfelt thanks to Manipuri Women players, Former-players, Association Office Bearers of Sports, Coaches of various games, sports journalists and SAI office bearers, who have served as the subject for the study. Without their cooperation and help the study would never have been completed.

I express my grateful thanks to Dr. Ksh Birbal Singh, Dr. L. Thambal Singh, Lecturer, D.M. College of Science and Manipur University, M. Megharaj Singh, Lecturer, Mount Everest College, Senapati, Manipur, L. Pungding, L. Bikram Singh, M. Suraj Singh, N. Suhindra Singh, Binita Basumatary, Ksh Rojeet Singh, students of Lakshmibai National University of Physical Education, Gwalior, P. Seema Devi, students of NIT Patna, Ksh. Deven Singh, for their help in the completion of the manuscript.

Last but not the least, I am grateful to Mr. M.P. Misra, Akansha Publishing House, New Delhi for undertaking publication of this work.

Y.S.S.

List of Tables

List of Illustrations

1

Introduction

Sports have a very prominent role in modern society. It is important to an individual, a group, a nation; indeed the world. There are, for example, today more nations compete in the Olympic Games than the number of nations affiliated to the United Nations. Throughout the world sports has a popular appeal among people of all ages and both sexes.

Much of the attraction of sports comes from the wide variety of experience and feeling that result from participation—joy, anguish, success, failure, exhaustion, pain, relief,belonging, and glory, status and goodwill. However sports can also bring tragedy, grief and even death.

Sports competition offers us heroes, heroines and ideal people that we can look up to, and achievement that we can marvel at; for many youth, sports stars are better known than the leading politicians of a country.

As the amount of leisure time has increased in modern society, time spent on sports has grown. While very few have been participating at elite or Olympic level there are many more who have been participants at the local or community level. For other, involvement in sports is passive one, as spectators, coach, umpires, teachers or sports writers or journalists. Sports have ever reflected development in society. Sports, indeed have been a mirror of society.[1]

Sports are the heart of many societies. It serves to improve life and the social order. The women sports start with conditions as they are, and moves forward goals both individual and society, of condition as they should be. It is one of the most constructive force in a society, and instrument by which people may fell themselves up and improve their ways of life.[2]

Sports are as old as the human society. Games and sports as apart of human education have always existed in human society in one form or the other. From time immemorial, physical exercise has been a very important aspect of human existence although it's not in a well organized fashion. In the primitive society, the necessity for survival motivated men to keep himself physically fit and strong. The "survival of the fittest" was the order of the day and therefore, his life was solely depends on his physical might and skill. Men lived in such a state for several millenniums. There was neither any Organization system. Most acts were learnt by young generation by virtue of imitation rather than instruction. Later on experience gave risk to individual instruction from the father to the son and mother to daughter.[3]

The changing role of women in society from the Victorian age to the present manifests an enormous social revolution, in which sports have played a major role and thus the development of women's sports in the present century definitely is one of the most fascinating topics.[4]

Sports reflect values found in our everyday lives and even in entire society. Women have been excluded from certain areas of significant participation in various aspects of living and this is also true for their involvement in sports and other physical activities. There is perhaps no domain were myths, attitudes and belief remain so persistent as in the world of sports.

There are myths related to females physical and psychological masculinization, the female's monthly cycle, pregnancy, the female's physical and psychological limits of performance capacity etc. most of these beliefs are rooted in long socio-cultural attitudes; however, there validity has not been demonstrated scientifically social approval is relative. It defers from era to era and from culture to culture within a era.

There are Nations which actively oppose any competitive efforts from women, other Nations urge their women to enter Olympic while still other merely permit them to do so. However, even today, some forms of competition are officially unexpectable for women as indicated by their exclusion from Olympic level competition. Perhaps an explanation for these attitudes could be found in the history of sports colored by male orientation and domination. Such a domination result from culture patterns and perception which determine not only who participated in sports, but also how the sports was to be conducted and experienced. However, today sports is seen as human activity, not just an activity more suitable for men than for women.[5]

Women, colloquially known as the better half of men are in reality his worse half. According to H. Sipla, "Half of the humanity that have yet to go long way to achieve quality of status and opportunity along with men. Equality between men and women does not exit. It is still often a disadvantage to be born a female. The historical evolution of human being has witnessed the ebb and flow of women's status.[6]

The traditional polarization of sex roles has produced in our society two different kind of human beings women and men, who are expected to play different roles, hold different attitudes, different value and express different feeling. Women are to assume role in the private sphere as wife, mother and home-maker, men are expected to assume roles in the public sphere as worker, citizens and active creator of social and cultural life.[7]

Traditionally, India had seen a woman only as a member of the family or as an individual with an indentity or right of her own. The radicalism of the constitution and its deliberate departure from the inherited social system lay in its implicit assumption.[8]

The females' participation in sports has been a cultural concern with a negative connotation. The socio-cultural milieu of each society somehow but invariably has webbed out certain constraint systems which desist women from participation in sports requiring physical power. In general, mostly it is considered appropriate that women are born for feminine role only and sports role fall out of this orbit. In relationship between the sexes, males have had a disproportionate amount of resources under their control. They could bargain their power, status, money, land, political influence, legal power and educational and occupational resources, (all usually greater than women's) against women's more limited range of resources consisting of sexuality, youth beauty and the promise of paternity. Men also could bargain their aggression, strength, strength, competitiveness and leadership capabilities against women's domestic and clerical services. In addition men could offer women potential maternity, reciprocally the ultimate validation of a women's feminity.[9]

In the few decades, women sports have gained tremendous popularity all over globe, which is still increasing at faster pace. Competition has become an important aspect of sports. Each country wants prove its superiority through sports at international level. For this they are making their most effort to fly high in national and international competitions.

Today in the modern competition sportsmen and women are in a race to excel each other and competition has become a fundamental mode. Human expressions as competitive sports are one of the very important factors for which international recognition and prestige are gained.

In India women activities or sports is growing and it is to make scientific and would be comparable to other modes of life, significant change have occurred throughout the world during the past quarter century. In yore days Indian women were discouraged to participate in sports. But today Indian women have earned more glory than their counterparts (men) in the field of sports.

The Manipur state is very small state, which locate in corner of north eastern region. The total populations of Manipur are 23, 88,634 and and females population are 1,181,296 only 23.88% are staying in urban area, other 76.22% were staying in rural area, and 59.70 of females are literacy.

Manipur is one of the states in India where games and sports are most popular. The people of Manipur are proud in the field of sports and games.

"Sports is the only area where the Manipuri agrees not to disagree." Nothing perhaps, sums up the enduring predicament of the athlete from Manipur, or even the northeast, better than this off the cuff remark by a local. The statement itself is loaded with contradiction. Because, sports has flourished in this strife-ridden state. Thriving despite violence, economic crisis and the centers blend eye on Manipuri people.[10]

Further the Manipur are proud of their girls in field of sports and games. And they have also the high attitude in participation of their girls and women, in various sports. The Explosion of women sports is amazing in National and international level. But Manipur state is still an under developed state in India. The state has very poor socio-economic condition, despite violence, less budget from centre, no sponsor from big companies, less facilities for sports, disturbance by Indian army due to Armed Forces Special Power Act, 1952, disturbance from Underground group. A professor of Manipur University point out the reasons why sports has come to mean the reason d'être for the youth from Manipur. "The state has been a case of urbanization without Industrialization. The agricultural sector too has been poor. Sports have become an industry and Manipur is seeking return from it. Apart from IT, Media, Sports is at the forefront of all this"[11]

The production of Sports women is very high in National and International level. So, on the basis the present sports scenario of Manipur and personal experience and knowledge, scholar wishes to find out the causes of popularity of women sports in Manipur.

Hence, the research scholar intends conducts an analytical survey, Manipur women are excelling in sports and games. In the survey the scholar have interact with all the people who had closely with women sports in Manipur.

The purpose of the study was to find out the reasons or causes of the explosion of women sports in Manipur.

Delimitation

The study was delimited to the Manipur women who have represented India or won medal in National championship in the following games/sports:

(a) Football (b) Hockey (c) Boxing
(d) Weight Lifting (e) Cycling (f) Judo
(g) Fencing (h) Fencing (i) Teak-won-do
(j) Athletics

ii) It was further delimited to the following people who have connected with sports in Manipur:

(a) Office bearer of Associations and Federations
(b) Coaches and SAI office bearers
(c) Former-Players
(d) Sports Journalists.

Limitation

(a) Some of the subject might have hesitation in confidentiality of response.

(b) Due to the lack of communication advantage questionnaire cannot be distributed to each and every corner of the state it is also considered as a limitation.

Definition and Explanation of the Term

Sports

1. It comes from “Disporter” meaning, “Carry away from work” a competition activity, pastime involving Physical Exertion.[12]
2. Sports an event held by a school or club at which there are games and competitions such as running, jumping and throwing.[13]

Explosion of Sports

The term means, that sudden increase or outburst in sports performance at National and International level.

Survey

1. It is the technique of descriptive research that seeks to determine present practices or opinion of a specific population taken from questionnaires, interview or normative survey.[14]
2. A descriptive study describes and interprets what is. It is concerned with conditions or relationship that exist, opinions that are held, process that are going on, effect that are evident, or trend that are emerging.[15]

Manipur

Manipur is a state of India, which is located in Northeastern Region, just at border of India and Myanmar. It is the state surrounded by Assam at West, Nagaland at the North, and Mizoram at the South.

Manipur is very small state, having a total population of only 23,88,634. The chief language of Manipur is Manipuri. The Loktak Lake, Keibul Lamjao and the Orchid yard at Khongampat, etc. are major attractions of tourist.[16]

Significance of the Study

1. The study may help in bringing out the fact and figures of women sports in Manipur.
2. The finding of the study may prove a source as a guideline to all who are concerned with women sports.
3. The study may aid in improving the standard of women sports in Manipur.
4. The study may help in popularizing women sports in the country.
5. The finding of the study may help for making policies and programmes of women sports.

6. The finding of study may help to find causes of poor performance as well as good performance in women of Manipur.

NOTES & REFERENCES

1 A.K. Uppal, *Foundation of Physical Education* (Delhi: Friends Publication, 1994), p.1.

2. Larson, *Foundation of Physical Activity*, p. 1.

3. M.L.Kamlesh and M.S.Sangral, *Principle and History of Physical Education* (Ludhiana: Prakash Brother, 1981), p. 10.8.

4. J.Bornns, M.Hebbelink and A. Vernerando, *Women and Sports* (S.Kargar Graphische Btriebe Coop Scheweiz. Basel 1981), p. 30.

5. *Ibid.*, p. 1.

6. Nisha Singh, *Women Education;* Women University News 38 (February 14, 2000)

7. Marry A. Boutilier and Lucinda San Giovavanni, *The Sport Women* (Champaign Human Kinetics Publish,1983), p. 100.

8. M.K. Singh, *Women and Sports* (Jaipur: Rawat Publication, 1990), p. 1.

9. A.T.Cheska, *Women's Sports—The Unlikely Myth of Equality, A Socio-pschyological and Kinanthropometric Approach* (Basel S. Karger 1981), p. 3.

10. Siddharth Saxena, The Sun always Shines on Manipur, (Sunday *Times of India*, 2007, 5th Feb. New Delhi), p. 22.

11. "The Sun always Shine On Manipur" (Santay Times of India, 25th Feb, 2007), p. 22.

12. Oxford English Dictionary, (Paper book Encyclopedia Entries, London) p. 776.

13. Macmillan English Dictionary, (Macmillan Publisher's Limited) 20006, pp. 1381-1382.

14. J.R. Thomas and J.K.Nelson, *Research Method in Physical Activity* (Human Kinetic, Publication 2001), p. 261.

15. Dr. M.L.Kamlesh, *Methodology of Research in Physical Education and Sports*, (Metropolitan Book Pvt. Ltd. 1986), p. 151.

16. *Manorama Year Book 2006* (Malayala Manorama), pp. 625-626.

2

Women Sports: Related Literature

A study of relevant literature is necessary to know the work done in the field of an analytical survey on women sports. The researcher has made every effort to locate and collect the literature relevant to this study from Newspapers, Journals and the available literature in the library of Lakshmibai National Institute of Physical Education, Gwalior. Brief reviews of the studies related to the present study which the present author has come across are cited below.

Rajiv Kumar[1] in his article says, as sports buffs across the country were watching the world cup, a group of around 20 girls from Barauni Flag village clad in football jerseys and shorts, were busy honing their skills at the village football field near Barauni in Bihar's Begusari district. One of them had even represented the country as part of the national women's football team in the women Asia cup in 2004 and 2006, held in China and Malaysia respectively.

Five of the girls are currently members of the state women's football team. And all of them hail from the same village. They undergo a grueling two hour practice session every day under the watchful eye of coach. Whether it is the mid-field dribbling skill of Annu, who play as stopper in the national team, their commitment of the game is clearly visible on the field.

Arjun Singh, a village elder says it all started 12 year ago. Sports lovers decided to form a village football team comprising women after a football match in which only women played was organized during the annual sports day celebration on January 14th 1994. Sadly, however, not a single girl has so far been able to get a job on the basis of her football skill. As a result the craze for the game is fast fading, said Singh.

Masusam, who has also had two years stint with the Mohan Bagan club of Kolkata in the Bengal women's league, say parents now consider it a waste of time and money for their children, particularly for girls to devote time to the game.

"With virtually no support from the state as well as from various district football Association, it will be hard to sustain the momentum," added by Mausam.

In fact, the neglect of local talent has not only left village sore, it has also prompted them to advise the new generation to concentrate on studies. Despite all this, they have constructed a stadium in the village comprising a football ground surrounded by grassy slopes on all sides so that villagers can sit and enjoy the game when their daughters "Bend it like David Beckham".

Report[2] of the Second All India Educational Survey on College and Institution of Physical Education by NCERT concludes, While the numbers of training institution are turning out increasing, it is generally felt that quality of the product is still far from satisfactory. This we gather is due to inadequate facilities and poor staff personal as well the different quality of the material that course for the training and the crowded syllabus that has to be covered in one academic year.

The Draft National Sports Policy[3] has did down the aims and objectives of new sports policy which are three-fold (a) to inculcate sports and health consciousness among the masses for regular participation in sports (b) to raise the standards in sports and in the process earn a place of pride in international sports competition (c) to provide all the necessary facilities and infrastructure which are essential for creating sports consciousness and promotion of the standard of performance in sports with a view to achieving these aims and objectives, the following steps have been prescribed to be taken:

Physical education and sports should be made compulsory in education institutions. Sports must become a compulsory feature of recreation in all factories and industries. Establishment of a network of rural sports centers.

Establishment of large numbers of sports clubs for urban youth. Holding of sports festival at district, states and national levels, yearly, two years and four years respectively. Indigenous sports like Kabaddi, Kho-Kho, and wrestling etc. to be developed and popularized. The mass media such as the Radio, T.V. and newspapers etc, should play more effective roles in promoting sports health consciousness and incalcating the habit of Physical exercises as a way of life.

The national physical fitness programme to be reoriented and implement more effectively. For spotting sports talents the district and state sports councils, the school game federation of India and district and state level units of the national federation should actively co-ordinate with each other.

The policy report also deals with existing government sports schemes. The All India Council of Sports, the Indian Olympic Association, the state sports council and welfare scheme for the sportsmen. The report highlights problem and drawback of the Indian sports and has provides some remedial measures.

Ayers[4] from his studies has concluded that parental attitude toward physical education were not related to socio-economic status parents considered the activities and the outcomes of Physical education programme either desirable or essential to the total educational development of the daughter.

Martin[5] has conducted a study to determine the attitudes of elementary school teachers and administrators toward athletics for female. Three hundred seventy three elementary school teachers and administrators were chosen. The result shows that (1) teachers and administrator disagree with items, which presented negative statement about female athletic agreed with items presenting positive views toward female athletes. (2) Teacher and administrators agree that a difference exists between the personalities of the female involvement.

Male teacher and administrators established a pattern of participating in sports, which have traditionally been reserved for man. (3) Teacher and administrator in this study could not be characterized by a particular pattern of attitude.

Sub-ground responses indicated that the certain subset of teacher and administrators were either more positive or more negative than other. It was concluded that elementary school teacher and administrator are a positive group toward female participation in athletic though teacher appeared more positive than administrators.

Ray[6] conducted a study in order to find out the attitudes of high school girls and their parents towards Physical education. The evidence indicated that the students who achieved high fitness scores and their parents viewed to contribution of physical education class for more favourable than did the students who were physically fit and their parents, and the parents and students differ in their view of the mental, emotional contributions. Parents and students for both groups had similar views about the physical psychological outcomes and the social contributions, while with regard to the emphasis placed on physical education in to total school programme. The parents of the low fitness group viewed this more favorable than their daughters. It was just the opposite with the high fitness group. Attitudes toward physical education were positively related to the senior high school girls achieved physical fitness score. A lower score regulated in a lower attitude towards Physical education.

Broer, *et al.*[7], in their article present the results of a survey of the attitude of 1,149 college freshmen women toward physical education as an activity. Study of total scores shows that they indicated a very favorable attitude. The student in swimming and tennis seem to have a more favorable attitude than average and those in archery a less favorable attitude. The high percentages of these students who indicate to social development, mental and physical health agree with result found at the University of Michigan.

Priyanka Kaushika's[8] article says as the countdown to the Commonwealth Games begins, why India lacks a sporting culture; Delhi is becoming with pride to host of Commonwealth Games 2010. India and advertisers keep remanding as how many days to go for the event. These are frenetic activity. All focus is on infrastructure and core is being investigated to meet international standard. But when it comes to playing the games, India is far behind in the international arena who is responsible for it? Parents, educational institutions, government or athletes.

Many feel that the interest in sports has to be encouraged from school through college and budding sports person need to be supported to perform better. Unfortunately, this is lacking in India. "Sports is getting sidelined in India." Admitted a senior official of the Central Board of Secondary Education (C.B.S.E.), adding we need to mainstream sports by making it compulsory subject. Only by giving it equal weightage as Maths and English will sports to be taken seriously.

Public schools have the infrastructure. Take for example Modern School on Barakhamba Road. It has two cricket fields, one football, two hockey, six tennis courts and four indoor badminton wooden courts. Sports practice takes place from 6-30 to 8 a.m. and during two period a week. Around 67 students excelled in different games of national level last year but they did not pursue sports as career.

The purpose of the Isenberger[9], study was to determine the relationship between the self attitudes of women physical education major students and those of women physical education teachers. Subjects used in the study were 277 women physical education student from three institutions and 167 women physical education Teachers. The "who am I?" test, a twenty statement test of self attitude (TST), was used as a measure of self-attitude. The result of this study indicated that there was a significant difference between the self-attitudes of students groups within a school and between schools. It was also indicated that the self-attitude of teacher differed significantly from those of students' enrolled in a liberal art university but were similar to those of students in teacher education institution.

Masse *et al*[10] in their article summarizes the finding of an exploratory meeting of 53 experts, brought together under the aegis of the women's health initiative to identify important issues related to measuring physical activity in minority women, in mid-life (aged 40-75) and older women (aged>75). The finding addresses five areas. Three dealing with measurement and two concerning the design of survey; (1) population characteristics to consider when measuring the physical activity of women and minority populations, (2) activity dimensions relevant to physical activity survey, (3) measuring moderate and intermittent activities (4) designing and administering Physical activity surveys for older and minority women, and (5) establishing the reliability and validity of such physical activity survey. Although the focus at the expert penal meeting was on identifying issues related to the measurement of physical activity in women, many issues summarized here can be generalized to children and men. The panel's finding concerning measuring physical activity are timely, as they directly bear on the challenges associated with the physical activity guidelines jointly issued by the American College of Sports Medicine and the recommendation made in the Surgeon General's 1996 report, Physical activity and health.

Elder *et al*[11] examined the influence of specific social interaction on immediate physical activity in children with data obtained from the behaviors of eating and activity for child health Evaluation system (BEACHES). The study examines parental and peer prompting of physical activity at home among 178 Mexican- American and 113 Anglo-American children at age 4 years and again at 6-5 years. Most activity prompts came from adult interacting with children when they were sedentary. A reduction in the frequency of prompts from baseline to follow-up occurred in the prompter group (adult or child peer), gender, ethnicity, and preprompted activity level categories. Children's responses to these prompts showed that as they aged, they seemed to rely less on the interpersonal (especially adult) aspects to their environment for cues to be more active.

Ballmann *et al*[12] in their study suggested that women participating in exercise, especially traditionally masculine activities, may experience pressure when trying to uphold societal image of the ideal female body. In addition women may feel obligated to maintain traditional female roles while conforming to societal views on female participation in exercise. This research suggest that the Physical Activity Acceptance Scale (PAAS) shows promise as a reliable and valid measure of individual perceptions of women who engage in traditionally masculine sports and exercise activities.

Nugent[13] conducted a study to provide voice for preadolescent females as they underwent an intense 2 year physical education (fitness and sports skill development) and self management intervention that was intended to enhance their attitudes toward physical activity while increasing their attitudes toward physical activity while increasing their activity levels. In both the fourth and fifth grades, the most frequently mentioned team participation outside of school. At the end of their fifth grade experience, five of the nine reported enjoying team activities.

Eyler *et al*[14] opined that despite decades of physical activity research and interventions conducted on men very little is known about the patterns of physical activity among U.S. women. They noted that rates from several national survey show much lower rates of physical activity for women than for men. Among women, rates may vary by socioeconomic status. Studies relating Physical activity and experience with heart disease, cancer; osteoporosis, and mental health are disused. Interventions in the work place and the community may increase the level of not participating in exercise and lack of time for this activity appears to be important constraints for many women. Applied research couple with community and workplace policies that support women's efforts to be more physically active may decrease the rate of some chronic diseases in this population.

According to Welch Suggs[15] Democrat or Republican, male or female, Americans strongly support equitable financing for men's and women's sports — even if that means cutting men's teams, according to a new poll commissioned by *The Wall Street Journal* and NBC News.

In the poll of 2,010 adults, 79 percent said they approved of Title IX of the Education Amendments of 1972, the federal law that prohibits institutions that receive federal funds from discriminating on the basis of sex in any program, including athletics. An additional 14 percent said they did not approve of the law; 4 percent said they did not know enough about it and 3 percent were not sure. In a separate question, 76 percent of respondents said they approved of "cutting back on men's athletics to ensure equivalent athletic opportunities for women," while 19 percent said they disapproved of such cuts and 5 percent were not sure.

The results did not vary much between different political and demographic groups. Seventy percent of Republicans said they approved of cutting men's sports, while 79 percent of Democrats did. Even men favored making athletics programs more equal, 73 percent to 22 percent, with the rest unsure. Women agreed, 79 percent to 16 percent.

"It's clear to me that the issue is on the top of people's minds," said David Iannelli, who with Robert Teeter conducted the poll for the Journal as part of a special section titled "Women, Politics, and the Marketplace." Another question on the survey asked whether women "count as much as men when it comes to" six social issues like becoming doctors and lawyers, making decisions about major purchases, and receiving financing for athletics programs. Only 14 percent said they definitely believed that women were receiving as much money as men, while 33 percent said that was sometimes the case, and 37 said that was not the case at all.

"When you take a look at parents and people getting used to seeing young women involved in athletics, that makes [the question of equitable funding] a non-issue," Mr. Iannelli said. He noted, though, that the poll did not ask specific questions about the economics of sports, such as the fact that women's athletics at the largest universities are often financed by revenues from football and men's basketball.

While Title IX does not require colleges to give the same amount of money to men's and women's sports programs or to have equal numbers of male and female athletes, it does require them to provide equitable resources and opportunities in a nondiscriminatory way.

The poll, conducted on June 14-18, had a margin of error of plus or minus 2.2 percent.

According to José Alfredo Flores[16], at the 1996 Summer Olympic Games in Atlanta, the U.S. women's basketball, soccer, softball and gymnastics teams brought home gold and set the stage for what's considered an explosion in women's sports.

Since "The Year of the Woman," as it was widely known, there has been a boom in women's sports coverage , from the 1997 launch of the Women's National Basketball Association to the 1998 U.S. women's gold-medal hockey team to the 1999 Women's World Cup Champion U.S. team. April 2001 will see the arrival of the Women's United Soccer Association.

Despite such overwhelming popularity, very few reporting beats were created to cover professional women's sports teams and women's sports in general. This lack of coverage was the central topic among the female sports journalists and athletes on a panel Thursday afternoon.

Newspapers continue to lag behind coverage on television and the Internet.

"The sports world is changing, and we're barely reflecting this," said Christine Brennan, sports columnist for *USA Today* and best-selling author of books on ice skating. "There is no excuse for this."

During the weekend of Feb. 12-13 this year, three sports events fought for television ratings. Tiger Woods was going for his seventh consecutive golf tournament victory at the Buick Invitational, the National Basketball Association was staging All-Star weekend and Michelle Kwan was favored to win the U.S. Figure Skating Championship.

Kwan won, but despite being a native of Los Angeles and a student at UCLA, her feat was reported on page 13 of the *Los Angeles Times* sports section.

"Why do I see figure skating all the time on TV and don't see it on the front pages of sports sections?" Brennan asked. "TV ratings are a measure of the popularity of the program, and newspapers do not reflect this."

Just six years earlier, the Tonya Harding-Nancy Kerrigan Winter Olympics rivalry brought figure skating to the forefront of the sports world. CBS' coverage of the 1994 Short Program in figure skating received a 48.5 ratings share, the sixth highest-rated program ever. The only other sporting events with better ratings were Super Bowls XVI and XVII. Despite the overwhelming increase in interest, no figure skating beats were created.

Niche publications were created to fill the void. "The explosion in women sports happened five years ago, but we're still waiting for coverage of this explosion," said Sandy Bailey, editor of *Sports Illustrated for Women*, which launched last month.

Much of the reason for thc expansion of women's sports involves Title IX, the 1972 law that requires federally funded institutions give equal support to men's and women's sports.

An example of Title IX influence occurred during last year's Women's World Cup, which brought more than 650,000 fans to stadiums across the United States during the tournament's 32 matches, with 40 million fans watching at home during the final.

Many of the team's players including Mia Hamm, the

world's most prolific female soccer scorer with 106 career goals were born about the time the law was passed. "They are the personification of Title IX," Brennan said.

"People don't see how enjoyable this form of entertainment can be," said Whitney Smith, who covers the Tennessee Lady Vols basketball team for The (Nashville) Tennessean. "The women's game doesn't have the flash of the above-the-rim game seen in men's basketball, but women should be allowed to display their talent."

Many female sports writers say editors who oversee their work tend not to cover women's athletics because the majority of their readers are businessmen, who have only recently shown any interest in these stories.

"With newspaper sizes getting smaller and others folding, it's a gamble to try something new," said Amy Shipley, Olympics sports beat writer for The Washington Post. "People cover what they are used to watching."

Susan Bischoff, deputy managing editor of the *Houston Chronicle*, says newspapers can't afford to ignore women's sports. "What many editors don't realize is that girls are interested in sports, and if they can't read about the WNBA or the U.S. women's soccer team in the newspaper, they'll find that information on the Web or elsewhere. In a time of dwindling circulation, newspapers cannot lose these potential readers."

Subsequently, many female sports reporters either change sections or leave journalism altogether. "Frustration, not the family, is the culprit," Bailey said.

Meanwhile several professional female athletes are upset that newspapers treat their leagues as second-class by sending interns, rookie or disinterested reporters out to cover their events.

"I can't tell you the amount of times when I had to go to a press conference and work to get [reporters] excited," said professional golfer Meg Mallon. "One time, a reporter told me that I was lucky that their paper was covering our golf event and that I better give them something to write about."

Cynthia Cooper, two-time most valuable player and three-time WNBA champion with the Houston Comets, said she is confused with teammate Sheryl Swoops during interviews. "I'm tired of being Sheryl," Cooper said. "Some journalists just don't care. They don't do their homework, and with the Internet it's so easy to find out about WNBA players."

F.Erik Lords[17], five years after settling a lawsuit that charged it with discriminating against female athletes, the California State University System is providing more funds, scholarships, and opportunities for participation in women's sports, according to a report released by the institution Tuesday.

Most of the system's campuses are in compliance with the terms of the settlement, and those that are not will be within a year or two, according to Ken Swisher, a spokesman for the system.

The changes are in response to a consent decree that settled a lawsuit brought in 1993 by the California chapter of the National Organization for Women. The lawsuit alleged that all of the system's campuses were discriminating against female athletes by not providing enough money for scholarships for women's teams, and by not offering enough opportunities for women to play sports. Cal State issued the report on its progress Tuesday in accordance with the terms of the 1993 decree.

"We're very pleased with the results of our internal report on gender equity in athletics," said John D. Welty, president of Cal State's Fresno campus and chairman of a committee that is monitoring how the consent decree is being carried out. "C.S.U. campuses have allocated massive resources to ensure equality of opportunity, and we will continue our commitment to this standard."

Linda C. Joplin, Cal-NOW's coordinator for athletics issues, said that she was pleased with the progress and that her organization would continue monitoring the system.

"C.S.U. has taken seriously its commitment to women's

athletics," she said. "Although all of the campuses are not quite there yet, the progress is significant, and their planning is sound."

Three campuses — California Maritime Academy, and the Cal State campuses at Monterey Bay and Channel Islands — were not part of the system when the lawsuit was filed, and the San Marcos campus did not have National Collegiate Athletic Association sports. Nineteen campuses are included in the report.

Some of the changes made between the 1992-93 and 1998-99 academic years: Financing for women's athletics jumped 266 percent, and financing for men's sports grew by 44 percent. Fifteen of the system's 19 campuses are now in compliance in this area.

Athletics scholarships for female athletes in the system increased by 184 percent; for men, the number of grants jumped by 59 percent. Currently, 49 percent of grants go to women in the system, up from 35 percent. Eleven of nineteen campuses are in compliance in this area. Participation opportunities increased as at least 38 new sports were added. Roughly 53 percent of all of the system's athletes are women, up from about 34 percent. Eleven of nineteen campuses are in compliance in this category.

Ebbeck et al.[18] studied the reason for adult participation in physical activity. An Interactional approach that simultaneously analyses personal and situational factors was employed to investigate why adults participation in physical activity. Specifically, this stud examined reason for participation by taking into account the interaction of gender and type of physical activity in which individuals were involved. Subjects included 422 adults who were enroll in university service physical education programme. The importance of various participation reasons was rated by individual involved in martial arts, swimming, tennis, volleyball, weight training and yoga. A factor analysis revealed that the participants engaged in Physical Activity for inter-dependence, personal satisfaction, self image and instrumental reasons. Further more, a MANOVA using factor scores as the dependent variable revealed a significant gender by activity interaction. The importance if interdependence as a reason for participation differentially varied for males and females across the six activities. Results of this study are discussed in terms of future research and practical implications.

Barnett and Wright[19] studied the psychological consideration for women in sports. They start with an overview of the expectations for women in the society may make participation in sports difficult for some, they then provide a psychological profile of the female athlete and highlight personality and mood difference that have been revealed between athletes and non athletes between more successful counter parts. Finally, they discussed a number of psychological problems that women athletes may experience, including identity issues, eating disorders, drug abuse, emotional responses to injuries, burn out and retirement.

Gill and Overdrof[20] investigated the incentives for exercise in young and older women, Two hundred and seventy two females between the ages of 18 and 16 years completed on exercise incentive questionnaire. Result showed that the youngest age group reported exercising significantly more as a means for gaining recognition then the 31-40 age groups. Physical health, fitness, stress management, task mastery and appearance were highly valued by subjects of all ages while competition and creative expression were the least valued incentive across the four age groups. The importance of mental health and affiliation as reason for exercise increased with advancing age. Sine incentives appeared to very by age exercise programmes must be structured to meet the goals of the specific participants.

Cash et. al.[21] investigated the factor structure and correlates of the reasons for exercise inventory among 101 exercising women. Subject completed the 24 item inventory (with one added item), reported their weekly frequency of exercise, and completed two standardized body image measures. Factor analysis indicated that with minor modification the instrument has an internally consistent structure with four factors of appearance or weight management was associated with a more negative body image independent of actual body mass and was the only motive related to self-reported frequency of exercise.

Rowe and Brown[22] in their article discussed a community based research project designed principles to encourage teenage girls to engage voluntarily in sports by improving local media coverage and developing the media and public relation skills of local sporting clubs and associations. The results also indicate that the importance of media coverage may be exaggerated and that media word of month and peer group encouragement are of much greater significance in actually raising sports registration levels among girls and women. The article concluded with a reflection that the project represents pointing to the need of diverse approaches to gender inequality in sport.

Zeelie and Potgeiter[23] studied the perception of female sports participation. Questionnaire were used to examine the perception of white high School pupils (N=540) and the self evaluation of adult white female sports participations (N=222) regarding the social desirability of their sport participation. The general attitude towards females sports participants them selves also feel comfortable with their sports roles. However, there is not a clear tendency with regard to sex role identification on the Bam (1974) scale. Difference in the perception of this sample, when compared with finding else where in the western would could be ascribed to cultural factors.

Henderson and Bialeshki[24] conducted a study by using two sets of qualitative data that addressed adult female participation and non-participation in physical recreation activities, typologies emerged concerning the way constraints were negotiated: achievers, attempters, compromisers, dabblers, and quitters/ defaulters. These typologies were depicted in a model that showed how women respondents to their constraints and the perceived benefits versus costs that were associated with physical recreation participation. The results have implication for examining trends in the negotiation of Physical recreation for further understanding the leisure and sport behavior of women.

Ryckman and Hamel[25] examined dispositional predictors of female adolescent involvement in organized team sports. Intrapersonal motivational variable, including affiliation, competition and achievement, were investigated as predictors of degree of sports involvement. Involvement was operational as the number of different sports played by these adolescents. Stepwise multiple regression analysis indicated that girls who had greater involvement in sports had stronger needs for positive stimulation through friendship and weaker needs for emotional support and attention than girls with lower level of involvement. Girls with higher involvement also had stronger competition attitude based on personal development goals. There was, however, no relation between hyper competitiveness (competing attitude aimed at self aggrandizement and opponent denigration) and sports involvement for these adolescents. The results were discussed primarily in terms of coach- athlete compatibility in attitude toward competition and their implication for the fulfillment of female athlete needs.

Smith[26] discussed parallel between women of color in society and sport. Although special emphasis is placed of Africa-America Women's historical and tradition information on other ethnic group socio- economic status and participation in sports is included. The discussion focuses on the absence or silence of diverse ethnic women with in the mainstream of society, sports and scholarship and summarizes literature that highlights intersections of gender race, and socio-economic class.

Fox, Corbin and Coulry[27] studied female Physical estimation and attribution to Physical activity. The psychological model for physical activity Participation and the physical estimation and attraction scales (PEAS) were developed by Senstroem using adolescent male subjects. This study investigated the adequacy of the model and instrument for explaining the involvement of college age females in model worked similarly for both- sexes, there were important difference. Attraction to physical activity, as measure by the attraction scale, dose not contribution to the model for the female in this study, but it dose for males. Physical estimation emerged as a key factor particularly for females, in its relationship with self esteem, fitness, and physical activity levels. The estimation scale appears to be a reliable and powerful instrument for assessing this construction.

Lever[28] studied the manner in which the sexes differ in play, as the tenth and eleventh years are reached. She found that girls play in smaller groups, play Outdoors less frequently, and play less often in competitive games than do boys. She also recorded that boys' games lasted longer, about 25 minutes, then girls' games; about 15 minutes was the longest girls game recorded in her survey.

Greendorf and Lewko[29] suggests that in college communities the father is a strong influence on the sport socialization of daughters.

Lenney[30] has proposed the notion of situational vulnerability. He has found, that women tend to lack confidence in achievement situation which are perceived as being sex role in appropriate.

Snyder and Kivlin[31] in a study on college athletes showed them to be more positive in their self-attitude than non-athletes.

Horner[32] published a highly influential paper which claimed that many women were motivated not by a need for achievement, or a fear of failure, but by a fear of failure, but by a fear of success, he also claimed that females were motivated to avoid success because this could negative consequences in terms of social rejection, decreased like hood of marriage, doubts about feminity etc.

Kapper[33] conducted a study on 739 college women students of Dilahoma University by administering an attitude inventory.

He concluded that college women had a favorable attitude toward physical Education.

Singh[34] in this article, "Why India Hockey Failed to score in World cup and Asian Games, spotted out the following reasons: The important reasons were lack of sufficient funds, artificial grounds, incentives to the player and coaches and above all, a lack of love for the game which brought our country so much glory. Besides this lack of good shooters, constant change strategies were the causes of poor performance. He said that constant change in the teams' coach has also become a disease. A coach should be given at least four years to prepare the side. He suggested that the coach should have full authority over the selection of the player.

Chapman[35] conducted a study to determine what, if any predictive qualities could be identified in a group of skilled women field hockey players. The specific areas investigated were anxiety, visual perception, manual dexterity, ball control, and dynamic balance, years of experience and playing position served as a secondary focus of experience and playing position served as secondary focus in the study. A total of 106 women field hockey players served subjects. The results from five tests, selected on the basis of a pilot study, supplied the data for analysis. The sport competition anxiety test (SCAT) a brief paper and pencil test, provided an anxiety measure. A modified version of Herlcoroity's Moving Embedded Figure Test (MEFT) was used to assess visual perception. Manual dexterity was determined by the two hand turning and placing test of the Minnesota Rate of Manipulation Test (MRMT). The Chapman Ball Control test (CBCT), a Test designed by the investigator was employed to assess skill ability in stick work. Dynamic balance was measured by the Scott sideboard leap Test (SSLT). Results indicated that dynamic balance, ball control, and anxiety were the discrimination variable for the group of selected women field hockey players. Visual perception and manual dexterity, as measured in the study, did not discriminate between successful and less successful field hockey players. Years of playing experience was not an important factor in group classification. Significant difference did exist between all control skill of goalies and field players.

Leslie in her article[36], mentions American athlete Ms. Morse was recently awarded a $35,000 grant to pursue training and coaching in England with a five-time Olympian. Ms. Morse competes in dressage, one of the few international level sports in which men and women compete equally against one another. After working her way from local competitions to national level events, Ms. Morse appears poised to reach the pinnacle of all athletics— the Olympics in 2004.

Ms. Morse began her competitive career on a $650 spotted Appaloosa. She has worked her way up through the ranks to win two United States Equestrian Team (USET) National Championships, and three United States Dressage Federation (USDF) Horse of the Year Championships.

Like most team sports, dressage requires more than one committed athlete. Ms. Morse has finally found the ideal teammate in a 17.2 hand bay stallion named Kingston. Although he has elegant long legs and powerful gaits, many in the dressage community did not believe Kingston had talent for international competitions until Ms. Morse forged a relationship with the horse. "I knew the moment I first sat on him that we would be a great team," Ms. Morse said. The pair has been virtually undefeated for more than two years and has won a USET National Championship and USDF Horse of the Year Championship.

Dressage is a sport much like pairs figure skating. Two athletes work as a team to demonstrate technical skills in an artistic setting, all set to music. Dressage has been an Olympic sport since 1912, and is a sport in which women consistently outscore their male counterparts; women have claimed the last four Olympic individual gold medals. Dressage is extremely popular in Europe and is one of the fastest growing equestrian sports in the U.S. To succeed in dressage an athlete must have strength, patience, and tenacity while preserving the spirit of the horse.

With the grant from the United States Equestrian Team, Ms. Morse was able to accomplish the lifelong goal of training with five-time Olympian Kyra Kyrklund. The time in Europe will enable Ms. Morse to establish an international presence. "In dressage, it is very important for the Americans to be seen by the international judges."

Thapar[37] conducted a study on the attitude and its effect on the performance of the competition. He suggests that to understand the word "Attitude", the Oxford dictionary says "it is a settled mode thinking". He says all the participants for the big event will not bear fruit if the players are not in positive mood on the day of the match. They should be full of confidence and eagerly await to show to the opponent as well as spectator they bent upon to fight till the last.

Singh[38] in his investigation suggest that one of the reason for poor performance by the players in our country is that we have not so far made our game and sports sufficiently science oriented. In this age of science we in India at the University level, are the least scientific in our approach to games and sports. Science analysis and assessment are not normally attempted. In the absence of critical evaluation of performance it is not possible fully to judge the performance of university.

Bajwa[39] in his thesis submitted to the Punjabi University Patiala on – An Analysis of the cause of failure of Indian Basketball team in the Asia Competition. The following conclusion were drawn after analysis the data; selection of the team is not done fairly and impartially non- technical and unfulfilled person are deputed as spectators while ignoring the game standard; political pressure and approaches are considered at the team for the Asia competition is done when competition comes very near. He feels that due to this reason the player do not get them combination and mutual understanding.

Raugh and Wall[40] conducted a study to determine the factors measuring sports participation motivation. Participation motivation factors were examined for university male and female athletes (n=59) members of physical education activity classes (n=10) and participants in intramural programmes (n=290). The questionnaire used discriminated among these three group with 75% accuracy and among these respondents classified highly, moderately, and unmotivated with 62% accuracy. Groups means were highest for athletes on each sub–scale. Response indicated that self-improvement, having fun and enjoying the activity and improvement of total fitness were most important.

Silva and Andrew[41] analyzed the game location and basketball performance in the Atlantic Cost conference (ACC). The performance of basketball teams participating in the ACC was systematically examined as a function of home versus away game location. The study was designed to determine if a home court advantage or an away court disadvantage existed in the ACC during a ten year period from 1971-1981. Performance indicators were field goal percentage, free throw percentage turn- over personal foul and rebound.

Descriptive results indicated that visiting team's loss more games and had a lower per game scoring average. Four of the five performances variables were found to be statically significant predictors of game location comparison of actual performance with ACC coaches' standards for performance suggested that an away court disadvantage existed for three of the four predictor variable. The rebound variable was the only performance indicator suggesting a home court advantage.

Kaur[42] conducted a study to determine the causes of poor performance of Indian Hockey at International Level. In this connection she investigated the opinion of Indian Hockey players and coaches regarding the causes of poor performance and its remedies. It was concluded that faculty and subjective election method; frequent change of coaches; inadequate technical and tactical preparation, insufficient match experience on synthetic playing surface, lack of proper diet; and lack of confidence, dedication devotion; discipline responsibility and fighting spirit by the players were the major causes of poor performance of Indian Hockey at international level.

Ogunjwenjo[43] conducted a study on the development of Nigeria's participation in International sports Competition and its effect on the nations, he included both individual and team games and the study was conducted on athletes, boxing, soccer, lawn tennis, Table Tennis, swimming, and team games of basketball and volleyball. The data was compiled from library, sources interviews of Nigeria. Data was collected from 300 athletes, coach and sport administrator. He found that the major weakness was in the area of inadequate facilities, insufficient personal, as well as ineffective planning for international sports competitions.

Long[44] determine which had the greater contribution to team success. Subject (n=47) from the SHS baseball teams, were administered a questionnaire to measure team cohesiveness; and three performance tests are administered to measure skills in baseball activity average calculated at the competition of the baseball season.

Linear regression analysis was used to compute S^2X, F-ratio and probability cohesion each subject evaluation of the team as a whole had a greater power of predicting success than the other two measure of cohesion concerning, each subject evaluation of every other team members and each subject evaluation of his relationship of the leans the skill measure throwing for accuracy had a greater power in predicting throwing for distance, speed and hitting ability.

NOTES & REFERENCES

1. Rajiv Kumar, "Village Girls bend it like Beckham" *Times of India*, July 16th, 2006.
2. Report of the All India Survey on College and Institution of Physical Education, *Educational Survey NCERT*, New Delhi, 1967
3. All India Council of Sports, *Draft National Sports Policy* (New Delhi: Ministry of Education and Culture, 1980)
4. Barara Ayers, "A study of parental Attitude Toward value of

Physical Education in Total Development of the Daughter" *Completed Research in Health, Physical Education and Recreation* 6 (1964) P.86

5. Eugene Curtis Martin, Analysis of the Attitude of Elementary School Teacher and Administrator Toward Athletic for Female, *Dissertation Abstract International* (Oct. 1979), p. 40
6. Barbara J.R, "Attitude of High School Girls and Their Parents toward Physical Education," *Completed Research in Health,* Physical Education 12 (1970):25
7. Marion R. Broer, Katharine S. Fox and Eunice Way, "Attitude of University of Washington Women Student Toward Physical Education an Activity," *Research Quarterly* 26 (Dec. 1955), p. 379.
8. Priyanka Kaushika, Give them a Sporting chance *Education Times,* 4th sept. 2006.
9. Wilma Isenberger, "Self Attitude of Women Physical Education Major Students and of women physical education teacher," *Research Quarterly* 30 (March 1959): 44
10. L.C. Masse et. at., "Physical Activity in Midlife, Older, and Minority Women: Issues from an Expert Penal," *Journal of Women's Health* 7 (1998):57
11. J.P. Elder et.al, "Direct Home Observation of the Promoting of Physical Activity in Sedentary and Active Mexican and Anglo-American children," *Journal of Development and Behavioral Pediatrics* 19(1998):26-30
12. Katie L. Ballmann, The Development of the Physical Activity Acceptance Scale: Determining Gender views on Female Participation in Traditionally Musculine sports and Exercise Activity," *Research Quarterly for Exercise and Sports* 68 (March 1997 Supplement): 98-A
13. Nugent, Preadolescent Females Preference and Attitudes toward outside School Physical Activities during a 2 year intervention", *Research Quarterly for Exercise and Sports* 68 (March 1997 supplement):34-A
14. A.A. Eyler et.al, "Physical Activity and women in the United States: An overview of Health Benefits, Prevalence, and Intervention Opportunities,", *Women and Health* 26 (1997): 27-

49

15. Welch Suggs, "Most Americans Favor Cutting Men's Sports to Add Women's, Poll Finds", (Chronicle of Higher Education Bulletin): Friday, June 23, 2000
16. José Alfredo Flores et. al, "Women's sports coverage still lacking, the *American Society of Newspaper Editors*,: 14 April 2000
17. Erik Lords, Increased Sports Opportunities for Women, the *Chronicle of Higher Education*, 2000.
18. Vicki Ebbeck *et al.*, "Reasons for Adult Participation in Physical Activity : An Internal Approach," *International Journal of Sports Psychology* 26(1995):262-275
19. N.P. Barnett and P.Wright, "Psychological consideration for Women and Sports," Clinic in Sports Medicine 13:2 (April 1994): 207-313 cited in *Sport Documentation Monthly* Bulletin 24:5 (May 1994):26
20. K.Gill and V. Overdorf, "Incentives for Exercise in younger and older Women" *Journal of Sports Behavior* 17; 2 (June 1994): 87-97
21. T.F. Cash *et al*, "Why do Women Exercise? Factor Analysis and Further Validation of the Reason for Exercise Inventory", *Perceptual and Motor Skill* 78.2 (April1994): 539-544 citers in *Sports Documentation Monthly Bulletin* 24:4 (April 1994): 24
22. Rowe D. and Brown A., "Promoting Women's Sports: Theory, Policy and practice," *Leisure Studies* (GBR): 3 Cited in *Sports Documentation Monthly Bulletin* 24 (January 1994): 37
23. Zeelei M.Potgieter, "Perception of Female sports Participation," *SA Journal for Research in Sports, Physical Education and Recreation* 14(1991): 77-82 cited in Sports *Documentation Monthly Bulletin* 23 January 1993):27
24. K.A. Henderson and M.D. Baileshki, "Negotiating constraints to women's Physical Recreation," *Society and Leisure* 16:2 (Fall 1993): 389-412
25. Ricard M. Ryckman and Jane Hamel, "Female Adolescents Motives Related to involvement in organized team sport" *International Journal of Sports Psychology* 23 (April-June) 1992:147
26. Y.R. Smith, " Women of color in society and sports," *Quest* (USA)

44 (August 1992) : 228-250 cited in Sports *Documentation, Monthly Bulletin* 22 (October 1992):28

27. Keeneth R. Fox, Charlos B. Corbin and William H. Couldry, "Female Physical Estimation and Attraction to Physical Activity," *Journal of Sports Psychology* 7 (June 1985): 125-136.
28. J. Lever, "Sex Difference in Games children Play," *Social Problems* 24:3 (1976): 478- 487 cited by Bryanth J. Cratty, *Psychology in Contemporary Sports: Guideline for Coaches and Athletes*, second edition, Englewood Cliffs, N.J. Prentice Hall Inc. 1983.
29. S. Greendorfer and J. Lewko, "Role of Family members in sport Socialization of Children," *Research Quarterly* 49(1978):146-152.
30. E. Lenney, "Women's self confidence in achievement Situation," *Psychology Bulletin* 84 (1977): 1-3
31. E. Snyder and J. Kivlin, "Women Athletes and Aspects of Psychological Well-being and Body Image," *Research Quarterly* 46 (1975): 191-199
32. Martina Horner, "Fail: Bright Women," *Psychology Today* 3(1969):36.
33. Eneline E. Kapper, "Inventory to Determine of College women Toward Physical Education and Students service of Physical Education Department," *Research Quarterly* 24 (March 1953);319
34. Balbir Singh, "Disasters of Today," *The Hindustan Times Sunday Magazine* (11th January , 1987)
35. Nancy L. Chapman, "An Investigation of the prediction of success in Women's Field Hockey," *Dissertation Abstracts International;* 40.4 (October 1979)1947.
36. Leslie Morse, "American Athlete Moves One Step Closer to Her Dream of 2004 Olympics" Google Search (internet)
37. K.D. Thapar, "Right Attitude Imperative for success in sports" *SNIPS Journal* (April 1981: 25
38. Karan Singh, "Study of Games and Sports Performance (men) of University of India Base on Inter- University Tournament Result of the Year (1981-82)" *University Sports* 5 (Sept;1982):101
39. Kamwaljit Singh Bajwa, "An Analysis of the Causes of Failure of Indian Basketball Team in the Asia Competition," Unpublished M.P.E. Thesis, Punjabi Unversity, Patiala, 1974.

40. Dorothy Raugh and Robert Wall, "Measuring Sports Participation," *International Journal of Sports Psychology* 18(1987):112

41. John M. Silva and J. Albert Andrew, "An Anlysis of game location and Basketball Performance in the Atlantic Coast Conference," *International Journal of Sport Psychology* 18(1987):188

42. Sukhdeep Kaur, "Causes of poor Performance of Indian Hockey at International level and its remedies" (Unpublished MPE Thesis Jiwaji University, Gwalior, 1987)

43. Ogunbiyi Daniel Ogynjivenjo, "The Development of Nigeria's Participation in International Sports competition and its effect on the National", *Dissertation Abstracts International* 39 (February 1978):784

44. Grant Long, "Cohesion: A predictor of team Success," *Completed Research in Health Physical Education and Recreation*, 15 (1973);126

3

Women Sports in Manipur: A Survey

In this chapter selection of subject, selection of Test, Selection of variable, Steps adopted in constructing the Questionnaire, Administration of Questionnaire and Statistical Techniques for analysis the data has been described.

Selection of Subjects

The subject for this study were selected at random from various parts of Manipur. For an analytical survey of explosion of women sports in Manipur, three hundred eighty subjects were randomly selected as the subject of this study. They are as follows:-

(1) One hundred women players who have represented India or won medal at National level in the following games and sports:

(a) Football (b) Hockey (c) Boxing
(d) Weight Lifting (e) Judo (f) Cycling
(g) Fencing (h) Teak-won-do
(i) Athletic

(2) Fifty Office Bearers of different Federation or Associations of Sports.

(3) One hundred former-women players of different sports.

(4) Fifty coaches of women's sports team of different sports. Fifty SAI office Bearers from Imphal.

(5) Thirty Sports journalists of Manipur.

Selection of Test

The selection of a proper tool was a vital importance for this study. They aim was to survey the Explosion of Women Sports in Manipur. For empirical analysis decided to use and self-made questionnaire as tool.

Selection of Variable

On the basis of available literature, observation and opinion gathered from the experts and under the careful supervision of the guide, the scholar located Three aspects which can influence the explosion of women sports in Manipur, the aspect are as follows:-

(a) Social Support

(b) Opportunity and Incentive Support

(c) Organization Functions & Sports Policy.

Construction of Questionnaire

The selection of a proper tool was a vital importance of this study. The aims were to survey the explosion of women sports in Manipur. The knowledge and experience scholars and expert of opinion was decided to use and self-made questionnaire as tool.

As it was survey study and the purpose of investigate were to find out the Explosion of Women Sports in Manipur. A self made questionnaire on topic was conducted and was employ to collect the necessary data. Forty one statements were prepared on the basis of three aspects of explosion of women sports in Manipur, namely: social support, Opportunity and incentive support, Organization functions & Sports policy. The majority of questionnaires were prepared by investigator himself with the help of his guide and other experts.

An attempt was made to make the working of the statement absolutely clear, relevant, simple and free from ambiguity, 1 to 41 statement of provision was made on right side of statement to note the respondent by (“) of the response, Yes and No respectively, which were to be recorded by ticking the appropriate statement according to their choice in the columns provided. Questionnaire also included open ended questions to allow the respondents to give response according to their own experience, knowledge, ideas, and observation about the wxplosion of women sports in Manipur.

A draft questionnaire was devised, observing the principle of questionnaire preparation. The Draft was scrutinized by different experts. After the scrutiny all meaningful suggestion was incorporated in the final draft of questionnaire of 41 statements.

Preparation of Test Item

The following procedure was adopted for the development of questionnaire.

Initial writing

In the first attempt a number of books, journals and sample questionnaires were consulted to frame various statements which required several responses. An attempt was made to prepare 85 statements in English language on the eight aspects of Explosion of Women sports in Manipur on which factors were selected; suitable change was made from time to time according to the instruction of the guide before the final draft was made.

Trial Run

After the formulation of the questionnaire, a tryout of the questionnaire was made. The purpose of this tryout was to discover whether the question was clear and adequate to obtain the information desired. During the tryout phase, the initial questionnaire was given to ten subjects of each group.

It was to find out whether the statement were easily understood and properly answerable. Taking into consideration the difficulties by experts the statement 46 items were eliminated.

Final Drafting/Re-writing

On the basis of guide evaluation the necessary change were made in the construction of questionnaire. On the basis of guide opinion two items were added to the questionnaire. Finally Forty One statements were drafted for the purpose of this study.

Items in Each Aspect

Questionnaire items in each aspect are given in the following Table:

Table – 1

Aspects of the Questionnaire

Sl.No.	*Aspects*	*Items No.*
1.	Social Support	1 to 19
2.	Opportunity and Incentive Support	22 to 29
3.	Organization Functions & Sports Policy	29 to 41

Administration of Questionnaire

The Questionnaire was administered to each subject with common questions. The researcher visited various areas of Manipur personally and assistant met all the subjects to collect the data. The scholar explained clearly in regional language about the purpose of the study along with how the questionnaire has to be completed (fill-up). The scholar also took help from Manipuri known person (assistant) to explain the statement in Manipuri. After ensuring the subjects had clearly understood the procedure of fill-up the statement. They were asked to record their response in the questionnaire.

Total of three hundred eighty questionnaire were administered among the 100 women players, 100 Former Players, 50 Sports Association office bearers, 50 Coaches of various sports, 50 SAI office bearers, and 30 Sports journalists.

The responses were received by Researcher on the basis of personal contact and through mailing. 370 responses were received out of 380 from the concerned subjects. Total 98% responses were received.

From the above subjects the particular subjects were responded are shown in the following Table.

Table – 2

Percentage of Responses Selected From Various Categories of Subjects

Subjects	*Total Admn. subjects no.*	*Total No. of Responded*	*Percentage of Responded*
Women players	100	100	100%
Ass. Office Bearers of Sports	50	50	100%
Former-Players	100	100	100%
Coaches and SAI Office Bearers	100	100	100%
Sports Journalist	30	20	67%

Collection of Data

The data were collected as per plan. Details of the research scholar's visit for purpose of the study and presented in the following Table-3.

Table – 3: List of the Places Research Scholar Visited for Data Collection

Sl. No.	*Dates of Visit*	*Places*	*No. of subject*
1.	18th.3.08 - 30.03.08	Bishnupur and Chunhandpur	50
2.	6. 6.08 - 15.6.08	Kakching	50
3.	17.6.08 - 30.6.08	Thoubal	50
4.	2.7.08 - 17.7.08	Imphal East	50
5.	20.7.08- 30.7.08	Imphal West	75
6.	15. 7.08- 25.7.08	Chandel	25
7.	11.6.08- 30.6.08	SAI Complex	80

Statistical Procedure

1) To assess the strength of the feeling of the subjects in each Statement the descriptive technique of percentage was used.
2) To find out the significant difference of the responses for Women Players, Former-players, Association Office Bearer of the Sports, Sports Journalists and Coaches and SAI Office Bearers, Chi-square test was applied. The level of significance was chosen at .05.

   The Formula[1]

$$X^2 = \sum [(O - \Sigma)^2 / \Sigma]$$

X^2 = Chi-Square

O = Observed Frequency

Σ = Expected Frequency

NOTE & REFERENCE

1. Jerry R. Thomas and Jack K. Nelson, "Research Method in Physical Activity" *Human Kinetic 2001*, pp. 167-172.

4

Women Sports: Analysis & Evaluation

In this chapter the analysis of data and finding of the study which was collected through administration of questionnaire has been described.

For the purpose of the present study data were collected from various sources. The main tool used for the collection of the data was questionnaire method. The questionnaire was sent to the Women players, Ex-players, Association office bearer of Sports, Sports Journalists, Coaches and SAI office bearers of Manipur and questionnaire consisted of 41 statements. The questionnaires were sent to three hundred eighty subjects through seven different groups of subject. Out of 380 questionnaires sent to subjects only 370 responses could be collected.

To assess the strength of feeling of Women players, Ex-players, Parents, Association office bearer of sports, Sports Journalists, Coaches and SAI Office Bearer on Explosion of Women Sports in Manipur, descriptive technique of percentage method was used, and to find out the significance difference between the responses of "Yes" and "No" of five selected subject groups, Chi-square test was applied at .05 level of significance.

Findings

Responses pertaining to each of the questions were analyzed and have been presented in terms of the total responses of percentage and Chi-square value. The findings of the present study are presented in the following tables.

Table – 4: Chi-Square Analysis of Opinion of Women players, Former-players, Association Office Bearers of Sports, Sports Journalists, Coaches and SAI Office Bearers on Social Support as reason of women's Sports Development in Manipur

Sl. No.	*Items*	*Subjects*	*Yes*	*%*	*No*	*%*	*Chi-Square*
1	2	3	4	5	6	7	8
1.	Social status of successful sports women encourae Manipuri women to seriously take up games and sports	Women Players	94	94	6	6	77.44
		Former-Players	80	80	20	20	36
		Assn. office bearers of sports	40	80	10	20	18
		Sports Journalists	18	90	2	10	6.8
		Coaches and SAI of office Bearers	93	93	7	7	73.96
2.	Manipuri Tradition and social environemnt is highly supportive for women sports	Women Players	88	88	22	22	57.76
		Former-Players	72	72	28	28	19.36
		Assn. office bearers of sports	36	72	14	28	9.68
		Sports Journalists	14	70	6	30	3.2
		Coaches and SAI of office Bearers	69	69	31	31	14.44
3.	Manipuri parents encourage their daughter to participate sports	Women Players	89	89	11	11	60.84
		Former-Players	85	85	15	15	49

		Assn. office bearers of sports	41	82	9	18	6.48
		Sports Journalists	20	100	0	0	20
		Coaches and SAI of office Bearer	96	96	4	4	84.64
4.	Manipuri folklore of heroic women also serves as an ideal motivating factor to take up sports by Manipuri women	Women Players	86	86	14	14	51.84
		Former-Players	72	72	28	28	19.36
		Assn. office bearers of sports	50	100	0	0	19.36
		Sports Journalists	18	90	2	10	6.8
		Coaches and SAI Office Bearer	89	89	11	11	51.84
5.	Manipuri women have equal right and dignified status like their men counterpart.	Women Players	100	100	0	0	100
		Former-Players	100	100	0	0	100
		Assn. office bearers of sports	50	100	0	0	50
		Sports Journalists	20	100	0	0	20
		Coaches and SAI Office Bearers	100	100	0	0	100
6.	There is no form of any social discriminaiton exist against women in Manipuri society.	Women Players	68	68	32	32	12.96
		Former-Players	59	59	41	41	3.24
		Assn. office bearers of sports	29	58	21	42	1.28
		Sports Journalists	19	95	1	5	16.2

(contd.)

1	2	3	4	5	6	7	8
		Coaches and SAI Office Bearers	80	80	20	20	36
7.	Parents provide every form of support required for sports participation and training.	Women Players	94	94	6	6	77.44
		Former-Players	97	97	3	3	88.36
		Assn. office bearers of sports	43	86	7	14	25.92
		Sports Journalists	18	90	2	10	12.8
		Coaches and SAI Office Bearers	95	95	5	5	81
8.	Structure and physical features of Manipuri women are suitable for sports	Women Players	93	93	7	7	73.96
		Former-Players	91	91	9	9	67.27
		Assn. office bearers of sports	49	98	1	2	46.08
		Sports Journalists	20	100	0	0	20
		Coaches and SAI Office Bearers	81	81	19	19	38.44
9.	For Manipuri women sports offers a secure career.	Women Players	73	73	27	27	21.16
		Former-Players	67	67	33	33	11.56
		Assn. office bearers of sports	33	66	17	34	5.12
		Sports Journalists	20	100	0	0	20
		Coaches and SAI Office Bearers	80	80	20	20	36

10.	Manipuri women take up sports for job security.	Women Players	54	54	46	46	0.64
		Former-Players	59	59	41	41	3.24
		Assn. office bearers of sports	25	50	25	50	0
		Sports Journalists	8	40	12	60	0.8
		Coaches and SAI Office Bearers	59	59	41	41	3.24
11.	Manipuri societies have culture and tradition of sports participation.	Women Players	88	88	12	12	57.76
		Former-Players	72	72	28	28	19.36
		Assn. office bearers of sports	36	72	14	28	9.68
		Sports Journalists	14	70	6	30	3.2
		Coaches and SAI Office Bearer	69	69	31	31	14.44
12..	In state of Manipur sports provide better employment scope.	Women Players	64	64	36	36	7.84
		Former-Players	68	68	32	32	12.96
		Assn. office bearers of sports	32	64	18	36	3.92
		Sports Journalists	17	85	3	15	9.8
		Coaches and SAI Office Bearers	82	82	18	18	40.96
13.	Manipuri sports women are more successful than their counterpart sportsmen.	Women Players	91	91	9	9	67.24
		Former-Players	86	86	14	14	28.88
		Assn. office bearers of sports	44	88	6	12	12.8

(contd.)

1	2	3	4	5	6	7	8
		Sports Journalists	18	90	2	10	60.84
		Coaches and SAI Office Bearers	89	89	11	11	17.64
14.	Manipuri sports women are dominating Indian women sports.	Women Players	71	71	29	29	4
		Former-Players	60	60	40	40	38.72
		Assn. office bearers of sports	47	94	3	6	3.2
		Sports Journalists	14	70	6	30	54.76
		Coaches and SAI Office Bearers	87	87	13	13	
15.	The success of Manipuri women at National and International have encouraged other Manipuri women to take up sports.	Women Players	100	100	0	0	100
		Former-Players	100	100	0	0	100
		Assn. office bearers of sports	50	100	0	0	50
		Sports Journalists	20	100	0	0	20
		Coaches and SAI Office Bearers	100	100	0	0	100
16.	Sports women like N. Kunjarani Devi are idol for Manipuri women.	Women Players	100	100	0	0	100
		Former-Players	100	100	0	0	100
		Assn. office bearers of sports	50	100	0	0	50
		Sports Journalists	20	100	0	0	20

		Coaches and SAI Office Bearers	100	100	0	0	100
17.	Given an opportunity Manipuri women will prefer other profession over sports	Women Players	62	62	38	38	5.76
		Former-Players	79	79	2	21	33.64
		Assn. office bearers of sports	37	74	13	26	11.52
		Sports Journalists	16	80	4	20	7.2
		Coaches and SAI Office Bearers	82	82	18	18	40.96
18.	Sports is not popular among rural women.	Women Players	37	37	62	62	6.76
		Former-Players	49	49	51	51	0.04
		Assn. office bearers of sports	26	52	24	48	.08
		Sports Journalists	9	45	11	55	0.02
		Coaches and SAI Office Bearers	41	41	59	59	3.24
19.	Social recognition is one of the reasons for Manipuri women opting sports.	Women Players	64	64	36	36	7.84
		Former-Players	70	70	30	30	16
		Assn. office bearers of sports	28	56	22	44	0.72
		Sports Journalists	15	75	5	25	5
		Coaches and SAI Office Bearers	80	80	20	20	36

Tab $x^2_{.05}(1)=3.84$

From Table–4 of Chi-Square analysis of opinion of selected categories of subject it is clearly evident that on statement 1 "Social status of Successful sports women encourage Manipuri women to seriously take up games and sports." The divergence of opinion to the responses "Yes" or "No" are significantly high with Chi-Square value 77.44, 36, 18, 6.8 and 73.96 for five categories of subject respectively. The statement-1 also shows the significant divergent opinion between "Yes" and "No" have converged with the higher percentage toward "Yes" for all the five categories of subjects with parentage of responses 94%, 80%, 80%, 90%, 93% respectively. These implies that all the five categories were significantly of opinion that social status of successful sportswomen encourage Manipuri women to seriously take up games and sports.

Further Chi-Square analysis on statement-2, "Manipuri Tradition and social environment is highly supportive for women sports". The opinion of five selected subject groups were significantly diverged between response "Yes" or "No" with Chi-square value 57.76, 19.36, 9.68, 3.2, 14.44 respectively. The significant divergent further converged with majority percentage towards "yes" on the above statement. The percentage of "Yes" opinion for the five subject groups were found as 80%, 72%, 72%, 70%, 69% respectively. These finding implies that significant majority of Manipuri Women players, Former-players, Sports Journalists, Association Office Bearer of Sports, Coaches and SAI office Bearers are opinion that for women sports, Manipuri Tradition and Social environment is high supportive.

The opinion on Parental encouragement, the opinion of five selected subject groups was significantly diverged for responses "Yes" or "No" with Chi-Square value 60.84, 49, 6.48, 20, 84.64 respectively. These divergences were significantly converged toward "yes" opinion with majority percentage 89%, 85%, 82%, 100%, 96% respectively for the opinion of five selected subject groups. These finding signifies all the five subject groups overwhelmingly of opinion that Manipuri parents encouraged to participate in sports.

On Statement-4 that is the folklore of Manipuri women is a source of motivation for Manipuri women, the opinion of selected categories of subject were significantly diverged with Chi-Square value 51.84, 19.36, 50.0, 6.8, 51.84 respectively. Further significant divergence is converged significantly with higher percentage of opinion toward "Yes" for the all five subjects groups. The convergence of opinion on "Yes" was observe with 86%, 72%, 100%, 90%, 89% all five subject groups respectively. This finding shows all the five subject groups are clearly of opinion that folklore of heroic women is an ideal motivating factor for Manipuri women to take up sports.

Further Chi-Square analysis on Statement-5 "Manipuri women have equal right and dignified status like their men counterpart" the opinion of five selected subject groups were significantly diverged between response "Yes" or "No" with Chi-Square value 100, 100, 50, 20, 100 respectively. The significant divergence further converged with all percentage towards "Yes" on the above statement. The percentage of "yes" opinion for the all five subject groups were found as 100% respectively. This finding implies that significant absolute of Manipuri women players, Former-players, Sports Journalists, Association Office Bearer of Sports and Coach and SAI office bearers are of opinion that for Manipuri women have equal right and dignified status like their men counterparts.

On Statement-6 that is "There is no form of any social discrimination exist against women in Manipuri Society". The opinion of five selected subject groups were significantly diverged between responses "Yes" or "No" with Chi-Square values 12.96, 3.24, 1.28, 16.2, 36 respectively. These divergences were significantly converged toward "Yes" opinion with majority percentage, 68%, 59%, 58%, 95%, 80% respectively for the opinion of five selected groups. These finding signifies all the five subject groups overwhelming of opinion that there is no form of any social distimination excess against in Manipuri society.

The opinion statement-7 on "Parents provide every form of support required for Sports Participation and Training" the opinion of five selected subject groups significantly diverged for response "Yes" and "No" with Chi-Square value 77.44, 88.33, 25.92, 12.8, 81 respectively. These divergence was significantly converged towards "Yes" opinion with majority percentage 94%, 97%, 86%, 90%, 95% respectively. This finding implies that significant majority of Manipuri Women, Former-players, Sports Journalist, Association Office Bearer of Sports, Coaches and SAI Office Bearer are opinion that parents provide every form of support required for sports participation and training.

Further Chi-Square analysis on statements "Structure and Physical features of Manipuri women are suitable for Sports" the opinion of five selected subject groups were significantly diverged between responses "Yes" or "No" with Chi-Square value 73.96, 67.27, 46.08, 20, 38.44 respectively. The significant divergence further converged with majority percentage of on the above statement. The percentage of "Yes" opinion for the five subject groups were found as 93%, 91%, 98%, 100% and 81% respectively. These finding implies that significant majority of Manipuri Women Players, Former-players, Sports Journalist, Association Office Bearer of Sports, Coaches and SAI Office Bearers are opinion that structure and physical features of Manipuri women are suitable for sports.

On Statement No-9 that is the "For Manipuri Women Sports offer a Secure Career", the opinions of selected categories of subject were significantly diverged with Chi-Square value 21.16, 11.56, 5.12, 20, 36 respectively. Further of opinion toward "Yes" for all five subjects groups. The convergence of opinion on "Yes" was observe with 73%, 67%, 66%, 100% and 80% respectively. This finding shows all the five subject groups clearly of opinion that "for Manipuri women sports offer a secure career".

On statement-10 that is "Manipuri women take up sports for job security", the opinions of selected categories of subjects were significantly diverged with Chi-Square value, .64, 3.24, 0, .8, 3.24 respectively. Further significant divergent is converged significantly with highly percentage of opinion toward "Yes" for three subject groups i.e. Women players, Former-players, coaches and SAI office Bearer. The convergence of opinion on "Yes" was observe with 54%, 59%, 50%, 40%, 59% respectively. This finding shows three of the selected subject groups clearly of opinion that Manipuri women take up sports for job security.

Further Chi-Square analysis on statement-11 "Manipuri societies have culture and tradition of Sports participation". The opinion of five selected subject groups were significantly diverged between response, "Yes" or "No" with Chi-Square value 57.76, 19.36, 9.68, 3.2, 14.44 respectively. The significant divergence further converged with all percentage toward "Yes" on the above statement. The percentage of "Yes" opinion for the all five subject groups were found as 88, 72, 72, 70, 69 respectively. This finding implies that significant majority of Manipuri women players, Former-players, Sports Journalist, Association Office Bearer of Sports and SAI office Bearers are opinion that Manipuri societies have culture and tradition of sports participation.

From statement-12 of Chi-Square analysis of opinion of selected categories of subject it is clearly evident that on statement" in state of Manipur sports provide better employment scope". The divergence of opinion to the responses, "Yes" or "No" are significantly high with Chi-square value 7.84, 12.96, 3.92, 9.8, 40.96 respectively. Statement-1 also shows the significant divergent opinion between "Yes" and "No" have converged with the higher percentage toward "Yes" for all the five categories of subjects with percentage of responses 64, 68, 64, 85, 82 respectively. These implies that all the five categories were significantly opinion that in the state of Manipur, sports provide better employment scope.

Further Chi-Square analysis on statement-13 "Manipuri sportswomen are more successful than their counter part sportsman". The opinion of five selected subject groups were significantly diverged between responses "Yes" or "No" with

Chi-Square value 67.24, 51.84, 28.88, 12.8, 60.84 respectively. The significant divergence further converged with majority percentage toward "Yes" on the above statement. The percentage of "Yes" opinion for the five subject groups were found as 91%, 86%, 88%, 90%, 89% respectively. These finding implies that majority of Manipuri women players, Former-players, sports journalists, association office bearer of sports, coaches and SAI office Bearer are opinion that "Manipuri sports women are more successful than their counter part sportsmen".

On statement-14 the opinion on "Manipuri sports women are dominating Indian women sports" the opinion of five selected subject groups significantly diverged for responses "Yes" and "No" with Ch-Square value 17.64, 4, 38.72, 3.2, 54.76 respectively. These divergence was significantly converged toward "Yes" Opinion with majority percentage 71%, 60%, 47%, 70%, 87% respectively for the opinion of five selected subject groups. These finding signifies, all the five subject groups overwhelming of opinion that Manipuri sports dominating Indian women sports.

Further on the statement-15 "The success of Manipuri women at National and International have encouraged other Manipuri to take up sports". The opinion of selected categories of subject were significantly diverged with Chi-Square value 100, 100, 50, 20, 100 respectively. Further significantly with all of opinion toward "Yes" for the all five subjects groups were 100% respectively. This finding shows all the five subject groups absolutely opinion that the success of Manipuri women at National and International have encouraged other Manipuri women to take up sports.

Further Chi-Square analysis on statement-16 "Sports women like N. Kunjarani Devi are idol for Manipuri women". The opinion of five selected subject groups were significantly diverged between response "Yes" and "No" with Chi-Square value 100, 100, 50, 20, 100 respectively. The significant divergence further converged with all percentage towards "Yes" on the above statement 16. The percentages of "Yes" opinion for all five subject groups were found as 100% respectively. This finding implies that significant absolute of all five subject groups are opinion that sports women like N. Kunjarani Devi are idol for Manipuri women.

On statement-17 that is, "Given a opportunity Manipuri women will prefer other profession over Sports". The opinion of five selected subject groups significantly diverged for responses "Yes" and "No" with Chi-Square value 5.76, 33.64, 11.52, 7.2, 40.96 respectively. Further significant divergence is converged significantly with higher percentage of opinion toward "Yes" for the all five subjects groups. The convergence of opinion on "Yes" was observe with 62%, 79%, 74%, 80%, 82% respectively. This finding shows all the five subjects groups clearly of opinion; given an opportunity, Manipuri women will prefer other profession over sports".

Further Chi-Square analysis on statement-18, "Sports is not popular among rural women". The opinion of five selected subject groups were significantly not between "Yes" and "No" except women player and Coach and SAI Office Bearers, with Chi-square value 6.76, .04, .08, .2 and 3.24 respectively. The significant were not divergence women players and Coaches and SAI Office Bearers and other were divergence. Further converged with all percentage of "No" Opinion for the all five subject. The percentage of "Yes" opinion the above subject groups were found as 63%, 51%, 48%, 55%, 59% respectively. This finding implies that significant majority of selected five group of subject are opinion that "Sports is not poplar among rural women".

Further Chi-square analysis on statement-19 "Social recognition is one of the reason for Manipur women opting sports". The opinion of five selected subject group were significantly not between "Yes" and "No" with Chi-Square value, 7.84, 16, .72, 5, 36 respectively. The significant divergence further converged with all percent toward "Yes" on the above statement. The percentage of "Yes" opinion for the five subject

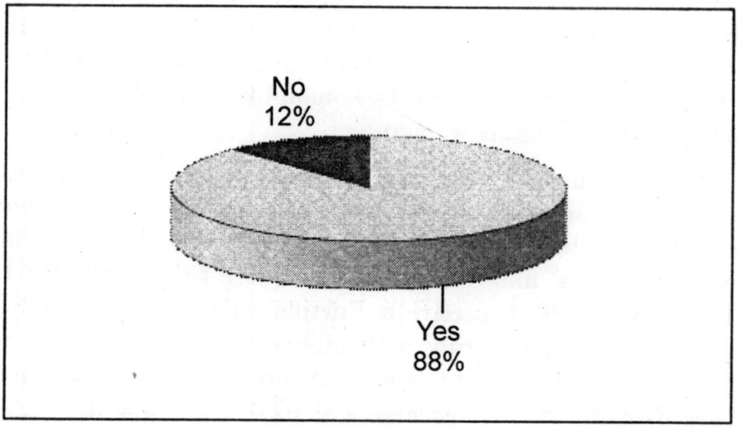

Fig. 1: Percentage Distribution on Social status of successful sports women encourage Manipuri women seriously take up games and sports.

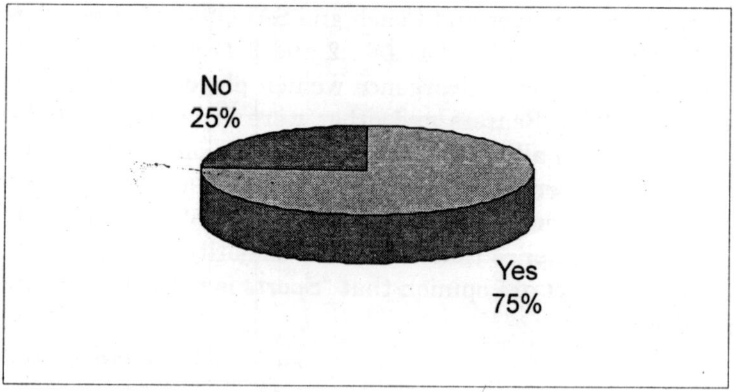

Fig. 2: Percentage Distribution on Manipuri tradition and social environment is highly supportive for women sports.

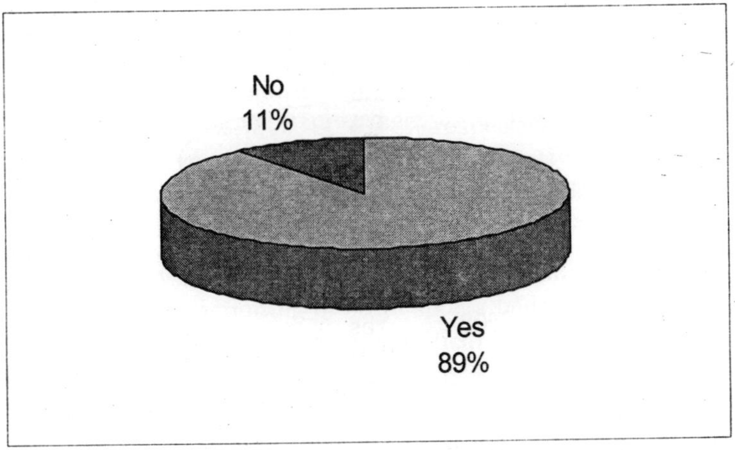

Fig. 3: Percentage Distribution on Manipuri parents encourage their daughter to participate sports.

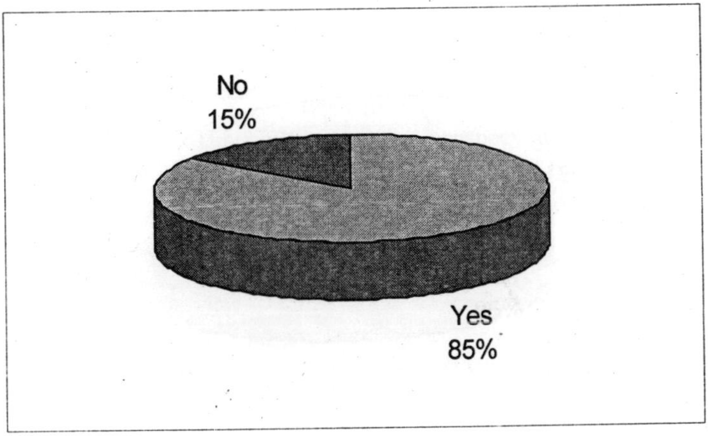

Fig. 4: Percentage Distribution on Manipuri folklore of heroic women also serves as an ideal motivating factor to take sports by Manipuri women.

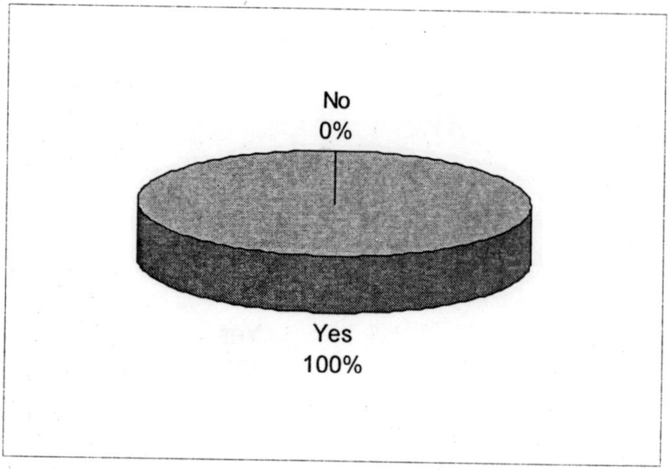

Fig. 5: Percentage Distribution on Manipuri women have equal right and dignity status like their men counterpart.

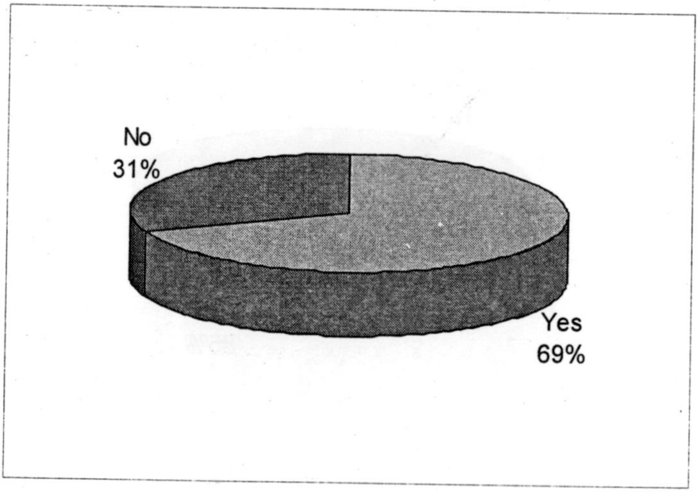

Fig. 6: Percentage Distribution on There is no form of any social dissemination excess against in Manipuri society.

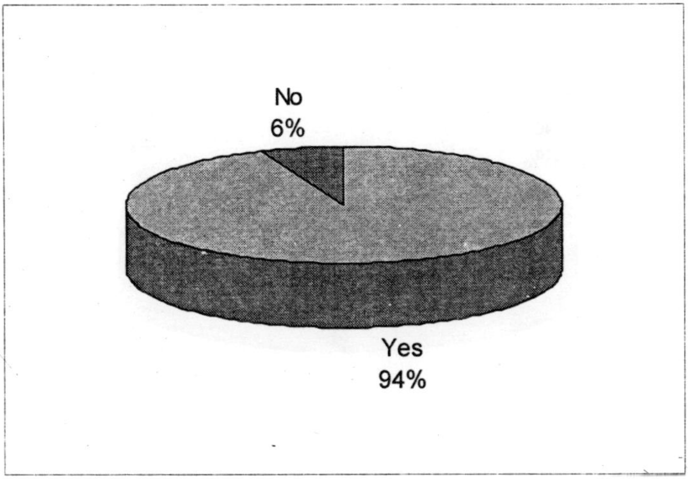

Fig. 7: Percentage Distribution on Parents provide every form of support require for sports participation in training.

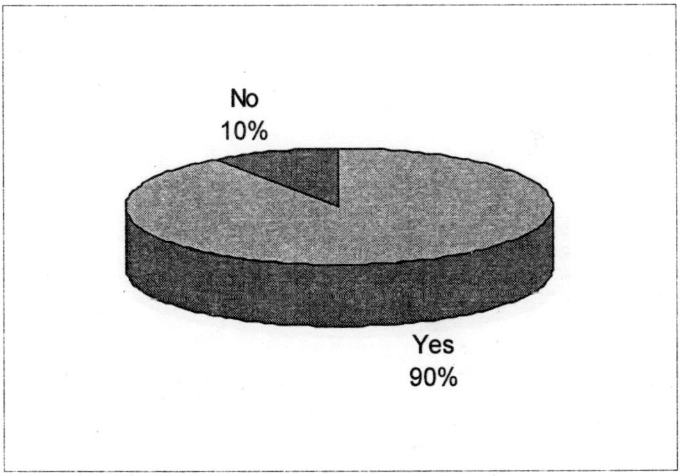

Fig. 8: Percentage Distribution on Structural and physical features of Manipuri women are suitable for sports.

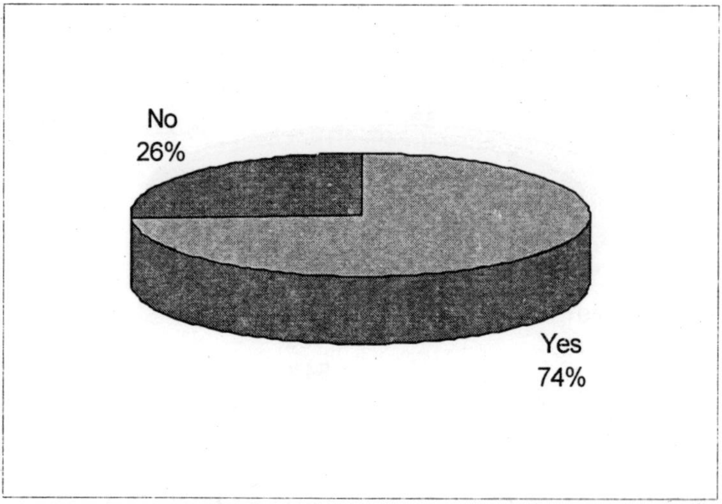

Fig. 9: Percentage Distribution on Manipuri women sports offer a secure career.

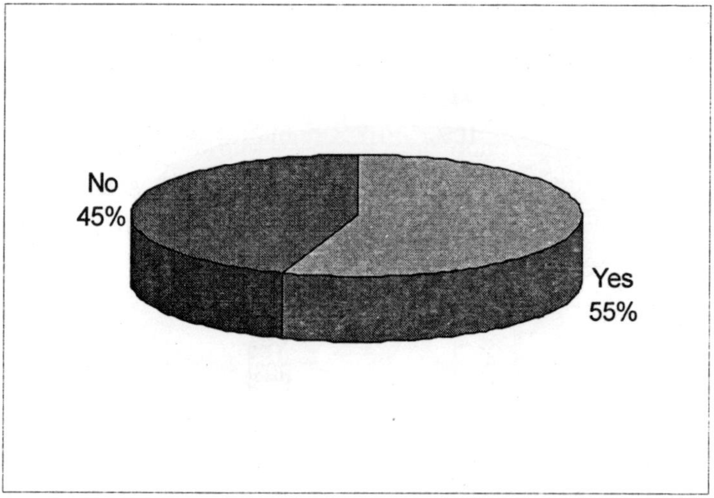

Fig. 10: Percentage Distribution on Manipuri take up sports for job security.

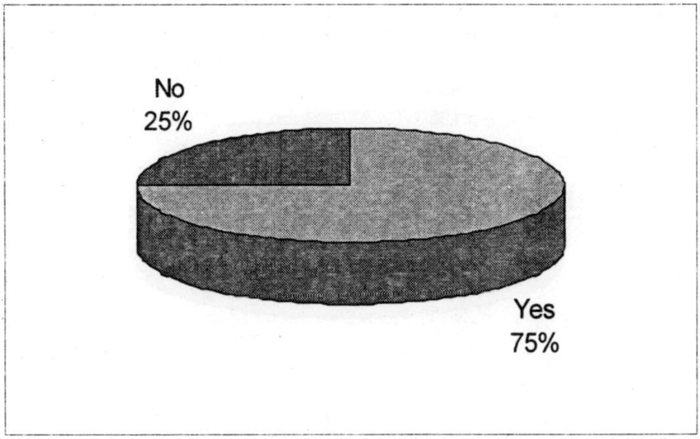

Fig. 11: Percentage Distribution on Manipuri societies have culture and tradition of sports participation.

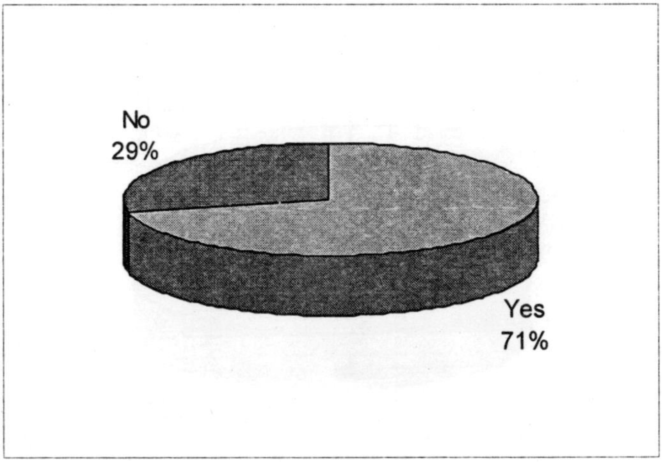

Fig. 12: Percentage Distribution on state of Manipur sports provide better employment scope.

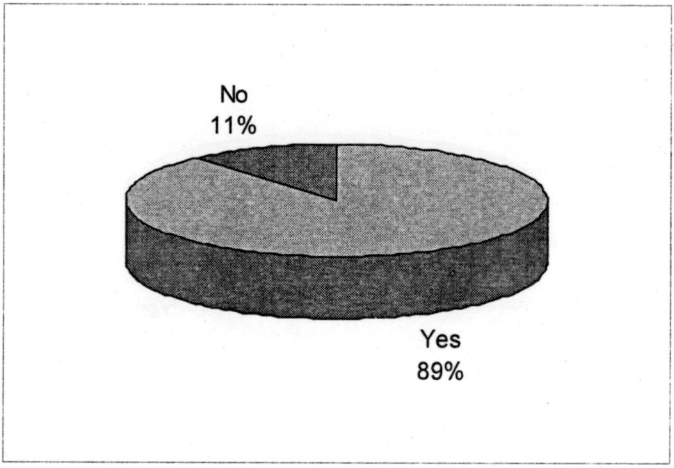

Fig. 13: Percentage Distribution on Manipuri sportswomen are more success than their counterpart men sportsmen.

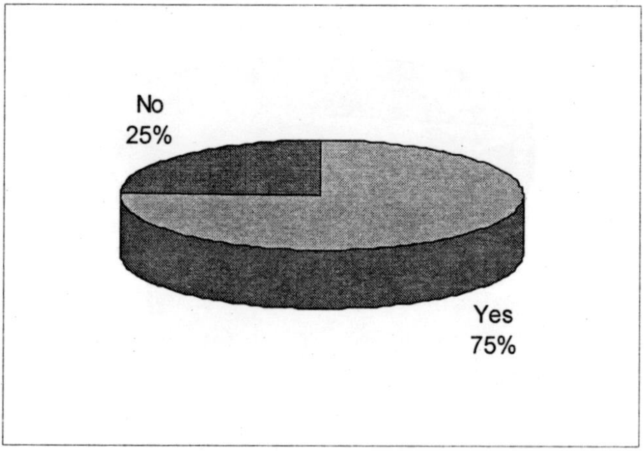

Fig. 14: Percentage Distribution on Manipuri sportswomen are dominating Indian women sports.

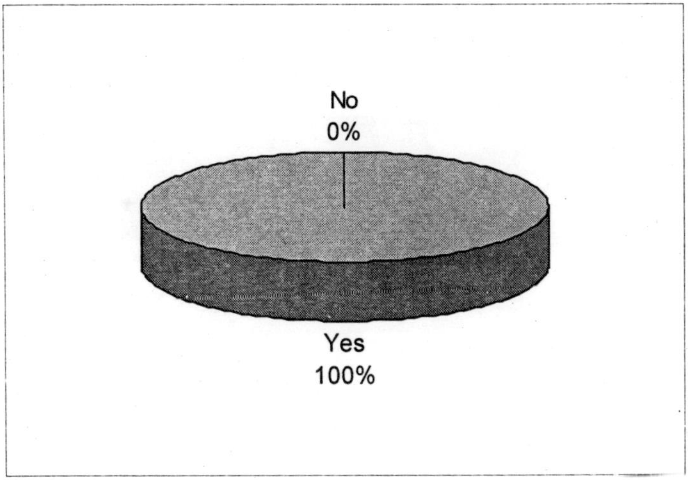

Fig. 15: Percentage Distribution on The success of Manipuri women at National and International have encouraged other Manipuri women take up sports.

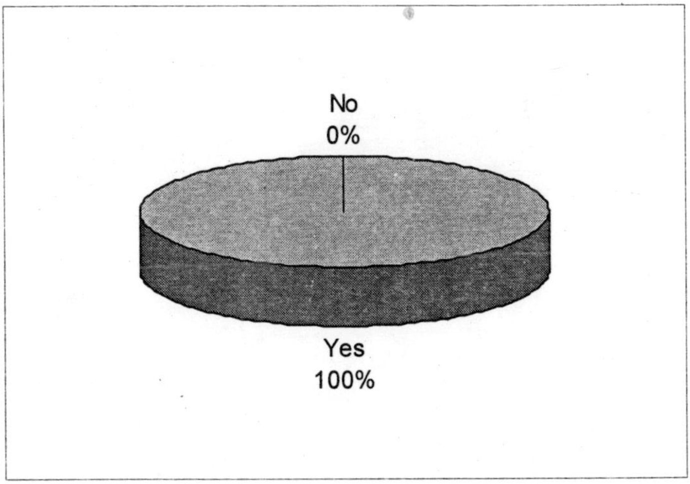

Fig. 16: Percentage Distribution on Sportswomen like N. Kunjarani Devi are idol for Manipuri women.

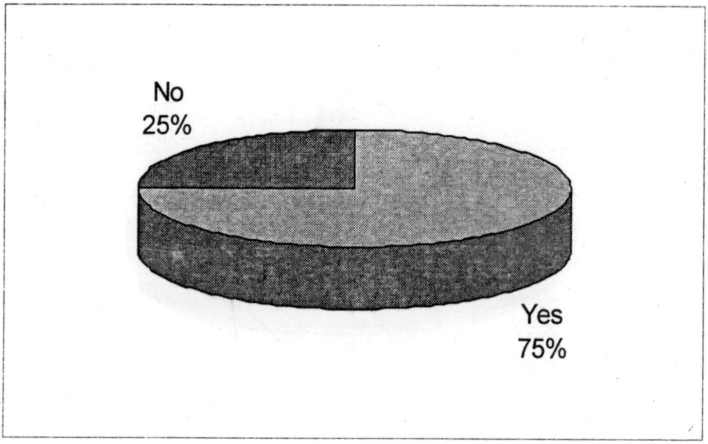

Fig. 17: Percentage Distribution on given a opportunity Manipuri women will prefer other profession over sports.

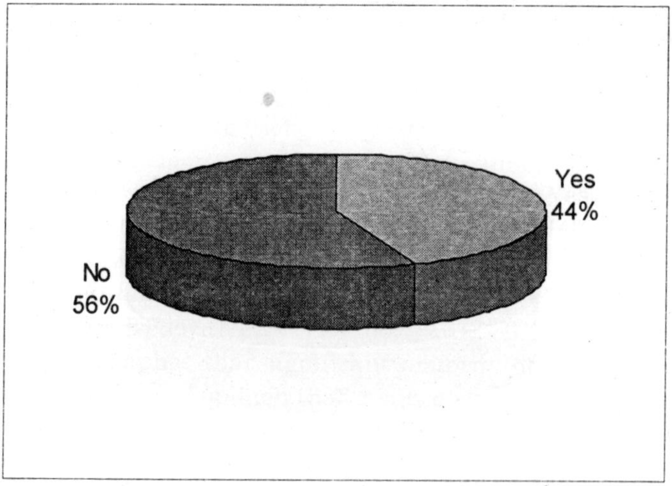

Fig. 18: Percentage Distribution on Sports is not popular among rural women.

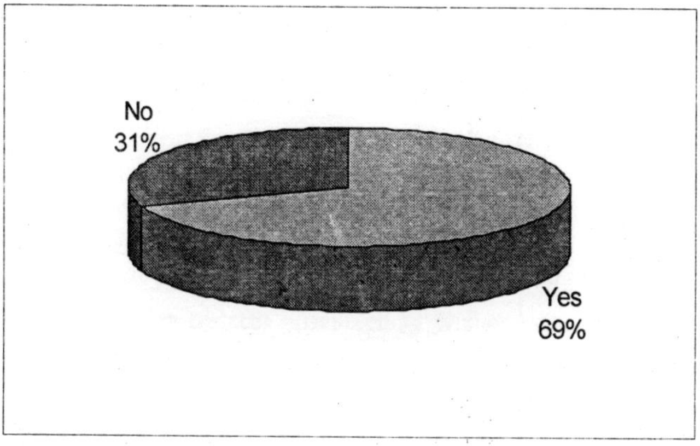

Fig. 19: Percentage Distribution on Social recognition is one of the result for Manipuri women opting sports.

groups were found as 64%, 70%, 56%, 75%, 80% respectively. This finding implies that significant majority of Manipuri women players, Former-players, Sports Journalists, Association Office Bearers of Sports and Coach and SAI Office Bearers are of the opinion that social recognition is one of the reasons for Manipuri women opting sports.

From Table-5 on statement-20, "The prospect of getting job is main reason to participate in sports". The divergence of opinion to the responses "Yes" or "No" are significantly high with Chi-square value 7.84, 12.86, 3.92, 9.8, 40.96 respectively. The significant divergent further converged with majority percentage of "Yes" opinion for the five subject groups were found as 64%, 68%, 64%, 85% and 82% respectively. This finding implies that significant majority of Manipuri women players, Former-players, sports journalist, Association Office Bearers of Sports, Coaches and SAI Office Bearers are opinion that the prospect of getting job is main reason to participate in sports.

On statement-21 that is, "Manipuri women participate in sports scholarship, financial support etc. from Govt.". The opinion of five selected subject groups significantly diverged

Table – 5: Chi-Square Analysis of Opinion of Women players, Former-players, Association Otrice Bearers of Sports, Sports Journalists, Coaches and SAI Office Bearers oon opportunity and incentive support for Women's Sports in Manipur

Sl. No.	*Items*	*Subjects*	*Yes*	*%*	*No*	*%*	*Chi-Square*
1	2	3	4	5	6	7	8
20.	The prospect of getting job is main reason to participate in sports	Women Players	64	64	36	36	7.84
		Former-Players	68	68	32	32	12.96
		Assn. office bearers of	32	64	18	36	3.92 sports
		Sports Journalists Coaches	17	85 and	3	15	9.8 SAI
		of office Bearers	82	82	18	18	40.96
21.	Manipuri women participate in sports for sports scholarship, financial support etc. from Govt.	Women Players	73	73	27	27	21.16
		Former-Players	91	91	9	9	67.24
		Assn. office bearers of sports	50	100	0	0	5 0
		Sports Journalists	19	95	1	5	32.4
		Coaches and SAI of office Bearers	83	83	17	17	53.56
22.	Availability of standard sports	Women Players	66	66	34	34	10.24

	facility encourage Manipuri women to take up sports	Former-Players	74	74	26	26	23.04
		Assn. office bearers of sports	37	74	13	26	5.12
		Sports Journalists	18	80	2	10	12.8
		Coaches and SAI of office Bearers	59	59	41	41	12.96
23.	SAI also have created good no. of sports facility.	Women Players	65	65	35	35	9
		Former-Players	79	79	21	21	33.64
		Assn. office bearers of sports	38	76	12	24	13.52
		Sports Journalists	12	60	8	40	8
		Coaches and SAI of office Bearers	83	83	17	17	43.56
24.	Compulsory Physical Education Programme in School and College have made significant contribution toward sports talent development at grassroot level.	Women Players	67	67	33	33	11.56
		Former-Players	77	77	23	23	29.16
		Assn. office bearers of sports	50	100	0	0	50
		Sports Journalists	10	50	10	50	0
		Coaches and SAI of office Bearers	67	67	33	33	11.56

(contd.)

1	2	3	4	5	6	7	8
25.	Availability of Sponsorship from National clubs etc. for better sports career and financial security for champions have greatly influenced Manipuri Women	Women Players	34	34	66	66	10.24
		Former-Players	40	40	60	60	4
		Assn. office bearers of sports	28	56	22	44	. 7 2
		Sports Journalists	11	55	9	45	. 2
		Coaches and SAI of office Bearers	45	45	55	55	1
26.	Central Government Agencies, like SAI's sports schemes have contributed in sports talent development	Women Players	77	77	23	23	29.16
		Former-Players	72	72	28	28	19.36
		Assn. office bearers of sports	39	78	11	22	15.68
		Sports Journalists	16	80	4	20	7 . 2
		Coaches and SAI of office Bearers	87	87	13	13	56.76

Tab $x^2_{.05}(1)=3.84$

for response "Yes" and "No" with Chi-square value 7.84, 12.96, 3.92, 9.8, 40.96 respectively. These divergence were significantly converged toward "Yes" opinion with majority percentage 73%, 91%, 100%, 95%, 83% respectively for the opinion of five selected subject groups. The finding signifies, all the five subject groups overwhelmingly of opinion that Manipuri women participate in sports scholarship, financial support etc. from Govt.

Further Chi-square analysis on statement-22, "Availability of standard sports facilities encourage Manipuri women to take up sports". The opinion of five selected subject groups were significantly diverged between responses "Yes" or "No" with Chi-square value 10.24, 23.04, 5.12, 12.8, 12.96 respectively. The significant divergent further converged with majority percentage toward "Yes" on the above statement the percentage of "Yes" opinion for 66%, 74%, 74%, 80%, 68% respectively. This finding implies that significant majority of all the five subject groups overwhelming of opinion that availability of standard sports facility encourage Manipuri women to take up sports.

On statement-23, that is SAI have created good number of sports facilities" the opinion of selected categories of subject were significantly diverged with Chi-square value 9, 33.64, 13.52, .8, 43.56 respectively. Further significant divergence is converged significantly with higher percentage of opinion toward "Yes" for the all five subject groups. The convergence of opinion on "Yes" was observe with 65%, 79%, 76%, 60%, 83% respectively. This finding implies that significant majority of Manipuri women players, Former-players, sports journalists, association office bearer of sports, coaches and SAI office bearers are opinion that SAI also have created good number of sports facility.

Further Chi-square analysis on statement-24 "Compulsory Physical Education Programme in school and college have made significant contribution toward sports talents development at grass-root level". The opinion of five selected subject groups significantly diverged for response "Yes" and

"No" with Chi-square value 11.56, 29.16, 0, 11.56 respectively. These divergence were significantly converged toward "Yes" opinion with majority percentage 67%, 77%, 100%, 50%, 67% respectively for the opinion of five selected subject groups. These finding signifies all the five subject groups overwhelming of opinion that is compulsory physical education programme in school and college have made significant contribution toward sports talents development at grass-root level".

The opinion is statement-25 "Availability of sponsorship from National clubs etc. for better sports career and financial security for champions have greatly influenced Manipuri women". The opinion of five selected subject groups significantly diverged for responses "Yes" and "No" with Chi-square value 10.24, 4, .72, .2 and 1 respectively. These divergence were significantly converged toward "No" opinion with majority percentage, except Sport Journalists, Association office bearers of sports, 66%, 60%, 22%, 9%, 55%. Further significant divergence is converged significantly with higher percentage of opinion toward "No" on the statement.

Further Chi-square analysis on statement-26, "Central Government Agencies like SAI" sports schemes have contributed in sports talent development. The opinion of five selected subject groups were significantly diverged between "Yes" or "No" with Chi-square value 29.16, 19.36, 15.68, 7.2, 56.76 respectively. The significant divergence further converged with all percentage toward "Yes" on the above statement. The percentage of "Yes" opinion for all five subject groups were found as 77%, 72%, 78%, 80%, 87% respectively. This finding implies that significant majority of Manipuri women players, Former-players, Sports Journalist, Association office Bearer of Sports and Coach and SAI Office Bearers are of opinion that Central Government Agencies, like SAI's sports schemes have contributed in sports talent development.

From Table-6 statement-27, "Is Politics in Sports organization have helped in effective functioning of sports organization" the divergence of opinion to the responses "Yes" or "No" are significantly high with Chi-square value 10.24, 23.04, 23.12, 12.8, 12.96 respectively. The statement 27 also shows that significant divergent opinion between "Yes" and "No" have converged with the higher percentage toward "Yes" for all the five categories of subjects with percentage of responses 66%, 74%, 74%, 90%, 68% respectively. This implies that all the five categories were significantly opinion that "Politics in Sports organization have helped in effective functioning of sports organization".

Further, Chi-square analysis on statement-28 "Are you satisfied with functioning of state sports body" the opinion of five selected subject group were significantly diverged between

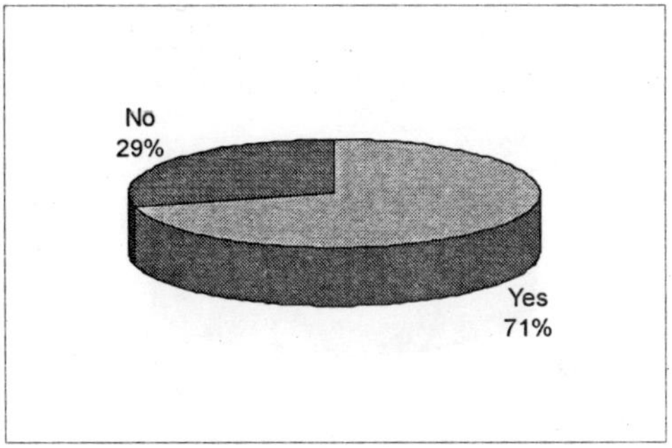

Fig. 20: Percentage Distribution on The prospect of getting job is main result to participate in sports.

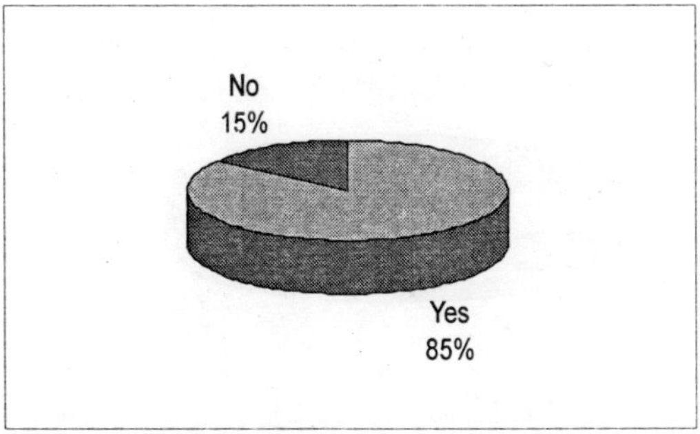

Fig. 21: Percentage Distribution on Manipuri women participate in sports appearing to seem sports scholarship, financial support etc. from govt.

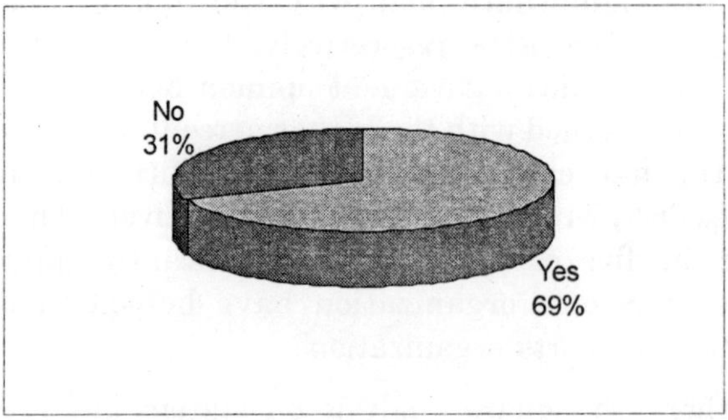

Fig. 22: Percentage Distribution on Availability of standard sports facility encourage Manipuri women to take up sports.

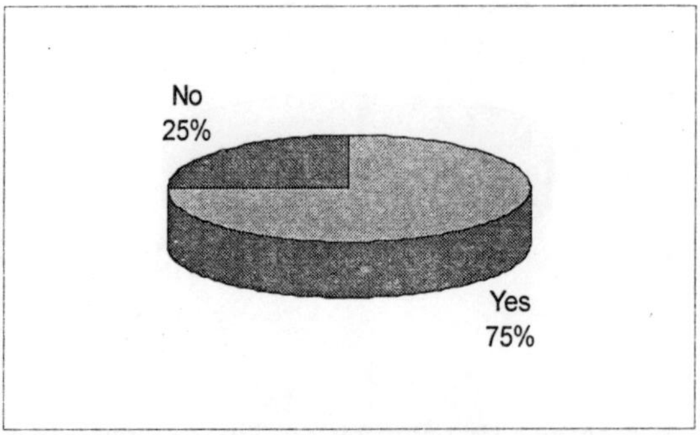

Fig. 23: Percentage Distribution on SAI also have create good no. of sports facility.

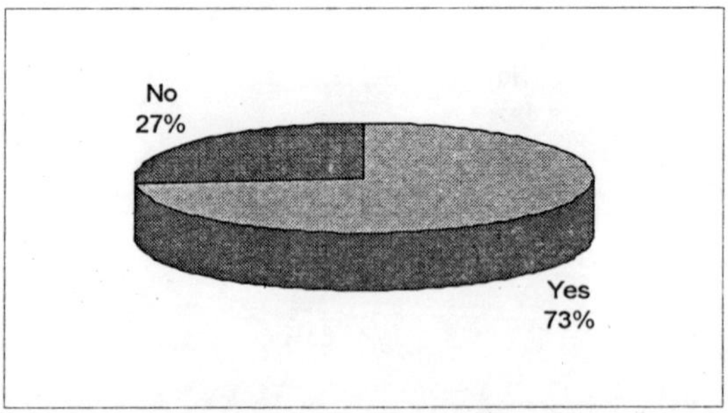

Fig. 24: Percentage Distribution on Compulsory Physical Education Programme in School and College have made significant contribution toward sports talent development at grass root level.

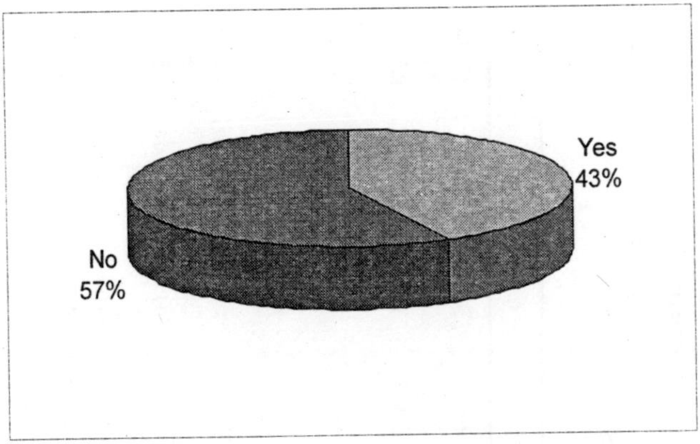

Fig. 25: Percentage Distribution on Availability of sponsorship from National clubs etc. for better sports career and financial security for champions have greatly influenced Manipuri women.

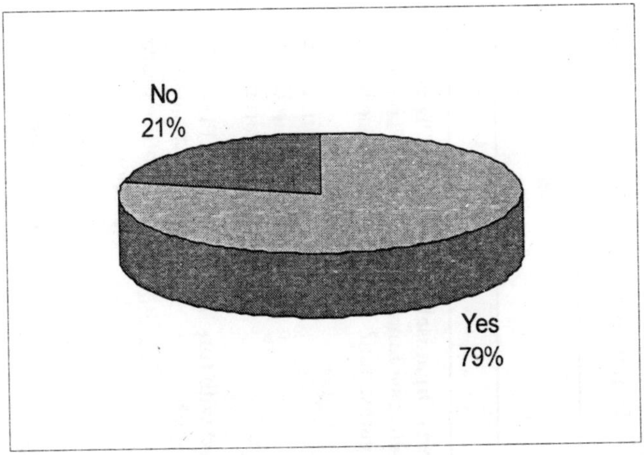

Fig. 26: Percentage Distribution on Central Government Agencies, like SAI's sports schemes have contributed in sports talent development.

Table – 6: Chi-Square Analysis of Opinion of Women Players, Former-players, Association Office Bearers of Sports, Sports Journalists, Coaches and SAI Office Bearers on Organization Functioning and Sports Policy as reason of Women's Sports Development in Manipur

Sl. No.	*Items*	*Subjects*	*Yes*	*%*	*No*	*%*	*Chi-Square*
1	2	3	4	5	6	7	8
27.	Is Politics in Sports Organisation have helped in effective functioning of Sports Organisation?	Women Players	66	66	34	34	10.24
		Former-Players	74	74	26	26	23.04
		Assn. office bearers of sports	37	74	13	26	23.12
		Sports Journalists	18	90	2	10	12.8
		Coaches and SAI Office Bearers	68	68	32	32	12.96
28.	Are your satisfied with functioning of state sports body?	Women Players	31	31	69	69	14.44
		Former-Players	70	70	30	30	16
		Assn. office bearers of sports	50	100	0	0	50
		Sports Journalists	10	50	10	50	0
		Coaches and SAI Office Bearers	58	58	42	42	2.56

29.	Are all games associations affiliated to National Federation?	Women Players	100	100	0	0	100
		Former-Players	100	100	0	0	100
		Assn. office bearers of sports	50	100	0	0	50
		Sports Journalists	20	100	0	0	20
		Coaches and SAI Office Bearers	100	100	0	0	100
30.	Are State Sports Associations used by Politicians for Political purpose.	Women Players	8	8	92	92	70.56
		Former-Players	12	12	88	88	57.76
		Assn. office bearers of sports	3	6	47	94	38.72
		Sports Journalists	1	5	19	95	16.2
		Coaches and SAI Office Bearers	16	16	84	84	46.24
31.	State Sports department regularly conducted inter-school sports competition	Women Players	64	64	36	36	7.84
		Former-Players	64	64	36	36	7.84
		Assn. office bearers of sports	48	96	2	4	42.32
		Sports Journalists	13	65	7	35	1.8
		Coaches and SAI Office Bearers	90	90	10	10	64
32.	Do you feel very few teams are sent to inter-university sports meet?	Women Players	54	54	46	46	.64
		Former-Players	65	65	35	35	9
		Assn. office bearers	38	76	12	24	13.52

(contd.)

1	2	3	4	5	6	7	8
		of sports					
		Sports Journalists	14	70	6	30	3.2
		Coaches and SAI Office Bearers	74	74	26	26	23.04
33.	Is more importance given to women sports for Manipuri Women's achieved records.	Women Players	54	54	46	46	.64
		Former-Players	59	59	41	41	3.24
		Assn. office bearers of sports	25	50	25	50	0
		Sports Journalists	8	40	12	60	.8
		Coaches and SAI Office Bearers	59	59	41	41	3.24
34.	State Sports Federation have played significant role in supporting women sports.	Women Players	67	67	33	33	11.56
		Former-Players	77	77	23	23	29.16
		Assn. office bearers of sports	50	100	0	0	50
		Sports Journalists	10	50	10	50	0
		Coaches and SAI Office Bearers	67	67	33	33	11.56
35.	State Sports Federation of Manipur works very efficiently.	Women Players	64	64	36	36	7.84
		Former-Players	68	68	32	32	12.96
		Assn. office bearers of sports	42	84	8	16	23.12
		Sports Journalists	17	85	3	15	9.8

		Coaches and SAI Office Bearers	82	82	18	18	40.96
36.	The success of Manipuri women are only due to support of Federation.	Women Players	48	48	52	62	16
		Former-Players	65	65	35	35	9
		Assn. office bearers of sports	47	94	3	6	38.72
		Sports Journalists	18	90	2	19	12,8
		Coaches and SAI Office Bearers	84	84	16	16	46.23
37.	State Sports Federations are corrupt and inefficient have done making for women sports.	Women Players	8	8	92	92	70.56
		Former-Players	12	12	88	88	57.76
		Assn. office bearers of sports	50	100	0	0	50
		Sports Journalists	1	5	19	95	16.2
		Coaches and SAI Office Bearers	16	16	84	84	46.24
38.	State Government have very strong sport policy to support women players.	Women Players	51	51	49	49	.04
		Former-Players	49	49	51	51	.04
		Assn. office bearers of sports	48	96	2	4	42.32
		Sports Journalist	2	10	18	90	12.8
		Coaches and SAI Office Bearers	58	58	42	42	2.56
39.	Is Political Environment supportive for development of	Women Players	59	59	41	41	3.24
		Former-Players	66	66	34	34	10.24

(contd.)

1	2	3	4	5	6	7	8
	sports.	Assn. office bearers of sports	44	88	6	12	28.88
		Sports Journalists	16	80	4	20	7.3
		Coaches and SAI Office Bearers	74	74	26	26	23.04
40.	Is insurgency resulted situation and environment have affected development of sports in Manipur.	Women Players	62	62	38	38	5.76
		Former-Players	71	71	29	29	17.64
		Assn. office bearers of sports	34	68	16	32	6.48
		Sports Journalists	12	60	8	40	.8
		Coaches and SAI Office Bearers	66	66	44	41	10.24
41.	Is Sports Ministry considered a important department in Ministerial Cabinet.	Women Players	100	100	0	0	100
		Former-Players	100	100	0	0	100
		Assn. office bearers of sports	50	100	0	0	50
		Sports Journalists	20	100	0	0	20
		Coaches and SAI Office Bearers	100	100	0	0	100

Tabl $x^2_{.05}(1) = 3.84$

response "Yes" or "No" with Chi-square value 14.44, 16, 50, 0, 2.56 respectively. The significant divergence further converged with majority percentage toward "Yes" on the above statement. The percentage of "Yes" opinion for the five subject groups were found as 31%, 70%, 100%, 50%, 58% respectively. These finding implies that significant majority of Ex-player, Association Office Bearers of Sports, Sports Journalists, Coach and SAI Office Bearers are satisfied with functioning of state sports body.

Further chi-square analysis on statement-29 "Is all games association are affiliated to National Federation?" The opinion of five selected subject groups were significantly diverged between response "Yes" or "No" with chi-square value 100, 100, 50, 25, 100 respectively. The significant divergence further converged with all percentage towards "Yes" on the above statement. The percentage of "Yes" opinion for the all five subject groups were found as 100% respectively. This finding implies that significant absolute of Manipuri Women players, Former-players, Sports Journalists, Association Office Bearers of Sports and Coach and SAI Office Bearers are of the opinion that all games association are affiliated to National Federation.

On Statement-30 "Is State sports association are used by politician for political purpose" the opinion of selected categories of subject were significantly diverged with Chi-square value 70.56, 57.66, 38.72, 16.2, 46.24 respectively. Further significant divergence is converged significantly with higher percentage of opinion toward "No" for all five selected groups. The convergence of opinion on "No" was observed with 92%, 88%, 94%, 95%, 84% respectively. This finding shows all the five subject groups clearly of opinion that state sports association are not used by politicians for political purpose.

On Statement-31 "State sports department regularly conducted interschool sports competition" the opinion of five selected subject groups were significantly diverged between response "Yes" or "No" with Chi-square value 7.84, 7.84, 42.32, 1.8, 64 respectively. The significant divergence further converged with all percentage forward "Yes" on the above statement. The percentage of "Yes" opinion of the all five subject groups were found 64%, 64%, 96%, 65%, 90% respectively. This finding implies that significant majority of Manipuri women players, Former-players, Association Office Bearers of Sports, Sports Journalists and Coaches and SAI office Bearers are of opinion that state sports department regularly conducted inter-school sports competition.

Further Chi-square analysis on statement-32 "Do you feel very few items are sent to inter-university sports meet?" the opinion of five selected subject groups were significantly diverged between response "Yes" or "No" with chi-square values .64, 9, 13.52, 3.2, 23.04 respectively. The significant divergence further converged with all percentage toward "Yes" on the above statement. The percentage of "Yes" opinion for the all five subject groups were found as 54%, 655, 76%, 70%, 74% respectively. This finding implies that significant majority of selected subject groups were of opinion that very few teams are sent to inter-university sports meet.

The opinion on the statement-33 "Is more importance given to women sports for Manipuri women's achieved records" the opinion of five selected subject group significantly diverged for responses "Yes" and "No" with Chi-square value 11.56, 39.16, 50, 0, 11.56 respectively. This divergence was significantly converged toward "Yes" opinion with majority percentage 54%, 59%, 50%, 40%, 59% respectively for the opinion of five selected subject groups. These finding signifies all the five subject groups. These finding signifies all the five subject groups of overwhelming opinion that Manipuri women's achieved records have given more importance to women sports.

Further the opinion on the statement-34 "State Sports Federation have played significant role in supporting women sports" the opinion of five selected subject groups significantly diverged for response "Yes" and "No" with Chi-square value 11.56, 39.16, 50, 0, 11.56 respectively. These divergence was significantly converged toward "Yes" opinion with majority percentage 67%, 77%, 100%, 50%, 67% respectively for the opinion of five selected subject groups. These finding signifies, all the five subject groups overwhelming of opinion that state sports federation have played significant role in supporting women sports.

The opinion on the statement-35 "State Sports Federation of Manipur works very efficiently" the opinion of five selected subject groups significantly diverged for responses "Yes" and "No" with chi-square value 7.84, 12.96, 23.12, 9.8, 40.96 respectively. These divergence were significantly converged toward "Yes" opinion with majority percentages 64%, 68%, 84%, 85%, 82% respectively for the opinion of five selected subject groups. These finding signifies all the five subject groups are opinion that State Sports Federation of Manipur works very efficiently.

On statement-36 "The success of Manipuri women are only due to support of Federation" the opinion of five selected subject groups significantly diverged for responses "Yes" and "No" with chi-square value-16, 9, 38.72, 12.8, 46.24 respectively. These divergence were significantly converged toward "Yes" opinion with majority percentage 48%, 65%, 94%, 90%, 84% respectively for the opinion of five selected subject groups except women players are of opinion that the success of Manipuri women are only due to support of federation.

On statement-37 "State Sports Federation are corrupt and inefficient have done making for women sports" the opinion of five selected subject group significantly diverged for response "Yes" and "No" with chi-square value 70.56, 57.76, 50, 16.2, 46.24 respectively. These divergence were significantly converged toward "No" opinion with majority percentage 92%, 88%, 100%, 95%, 84% respectively for the opinion of five selected subject groups. These finding signifies, all the five subject groups overwhelming of opinion that State Sports Federation are corrupt and inefficiently have making for women sports.

On the statement-38 "State Government have very strong sports policy to support women player" the opinion of five selected subject group significantly diverged for response "Yes" and "No" with Chi-square value 3.24, 10.24, 28.88, 7.2, 23.04 respectively. These divergences were significantly converged toward "Yes" opinion with majority percentage 59%, 66%, 88%, 80%, 74% respectively for the opinion of five selected subject groups. These finding signifies all the five subject groups are of opinion that State Government have very strong sports policy to support women players.

On statement-39 "Is Political Environment is supportive for development of sports" the opinion of selected categories of subject were significantly diverged with chi-square value .04, .04, 42.32, 12.8, 2.56 respectively. Further significantly with higher percentage of opinion toward "Yes" for the five subjects groups. The convergence of opinion on "Yes" was observe with 51%, 49%, 96%, 10%, 58% respectively. These finding implies that significant majority of five selected subjects groups are of opinion that political environment is supportive for development of sports.

Further Chi-square analysis on the statement-40 "Is insurgency related situation and environment have affected development of sports in Manipur" the opinion of selected categories of subject were significantly diverged with Chi-square value 5.76, 17.69, 6.48, .8, 10.24 respectively. Further significantly with higher percentage of opinion toward "Yes" for the five subjects groups. The convergence of opinion on "Yes" was observed with 62%, 71%, 68%, 60%, 66% respectively. This finding implies that significant majority of five selected subject groups are of opinion that insurgency related situation and environment have affected development of sports in Manipur.

Further Chi-square analysis on statement-41 "Is sports Ministry is considered a important department in Ministerial Cabinet" the opinion of five selected subject groups were significantly diverged between response "Yes" or "No" with chi-square value 100, 100, 50, 20, 100 respectively. The significant divergence further converged with all percentage toward "Yes" on the above statement. The percentage "Yes" opinion for the all five subject groups were found as 100% each respectively. This finding implies that significant absolute of five selected subject groups are of opinion that Sports Ministry is considered an important department in Ministerial cabinet.

Discussion of Finding

From elaborate statistical analysis of opinions of five categories of subject who are considered to be persons associated with women sports and could provide valuable information on women sports, many hidden and critical facts were revealed.

The very idea and purpose of study was to critically understand the parts underlines growth and popularity of women sports in Manipur, Rcsearch scholar feel the finding of study has accomplished successfully the very idea and all the objectives of the study.

The opinion of reliable subjects of five group as Women players, Former-players, Association Office Bearers of Sports, Sports Journalists, Coaches and SAI office bearers were analyzed under these categories. The categories were social supports opportunity and incentive supports, organization functioning and support policy.

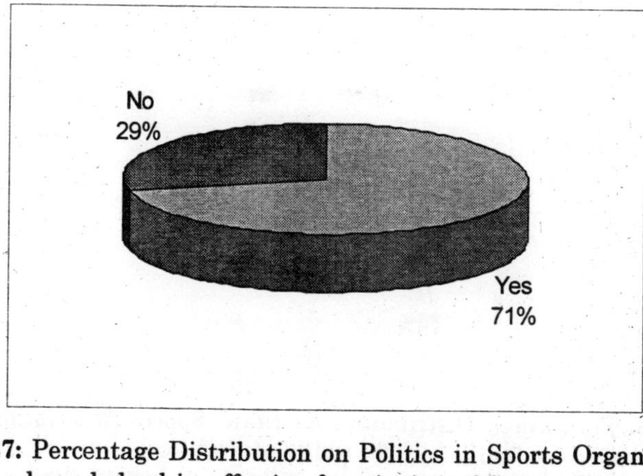

Fig. 27: Percentage Distribution on Politics in Sports Organisation have helped in effective functioning of Sports Organisation

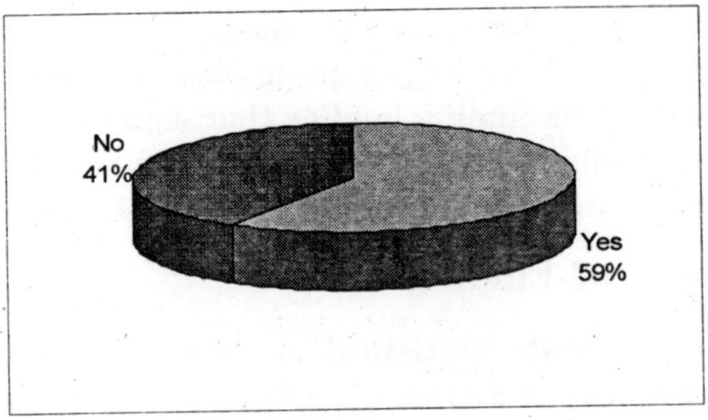

Fig. 28: Percentage Distribution on satisfied with functioning of state sports body

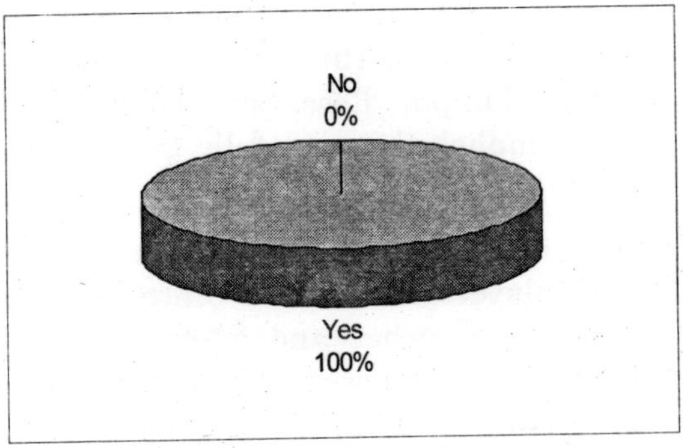

Fig. 29: Percentage Distribution on games association are affiliated to National Federation

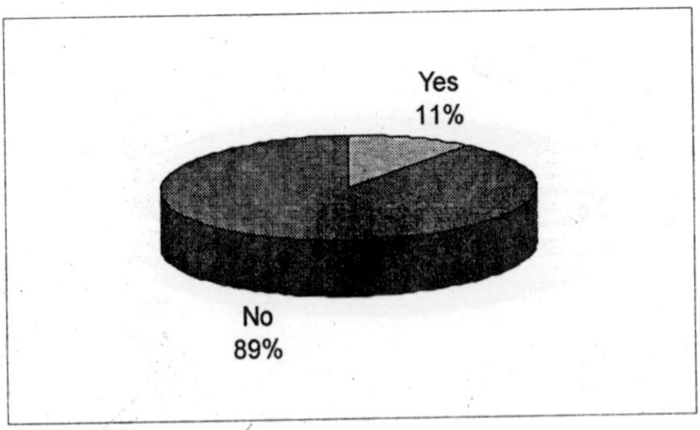

Fig. 30: Percentage Distribution on State Sports Associations are used by Politicians for political purpose.

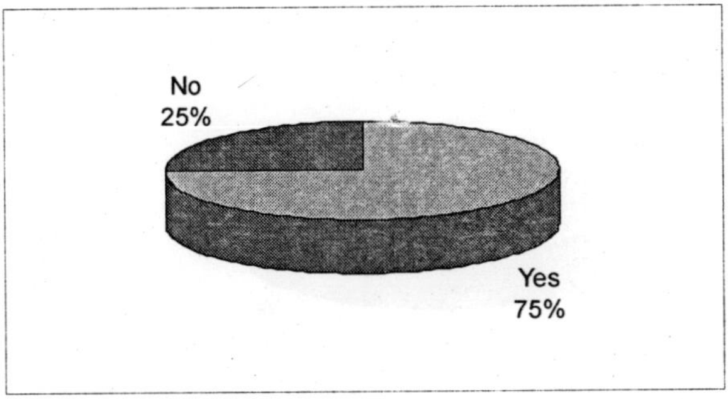

Fig. 31: Percentage Distribution on State Sports department **regularly** conducted inter-school sports competition.

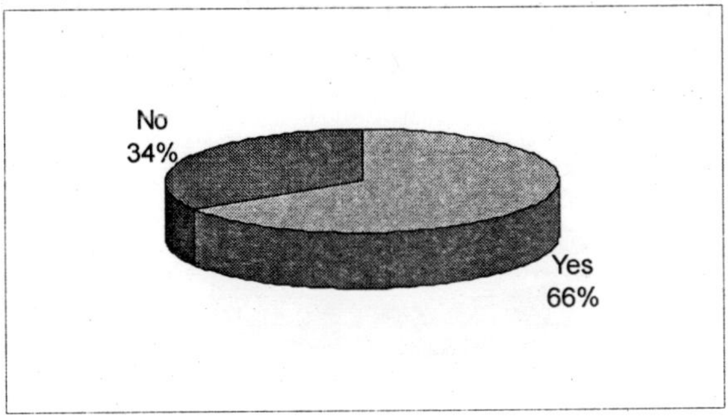

Fig. 32: Percentage Distribution on few teams are sent to **inter-**university sports meet.

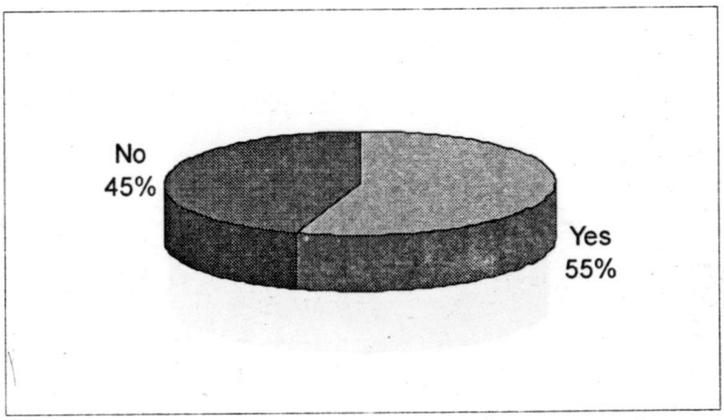

Fig. 33: Percentage Distribution on importance is given to wome: sports for Manipuri Women's achieved records.

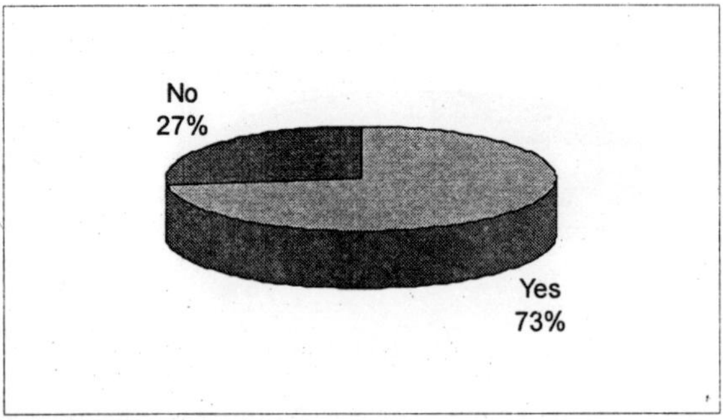

Fig. 34: Percentage Distribution on State Sports Federation have played significant role in supporting women sports.

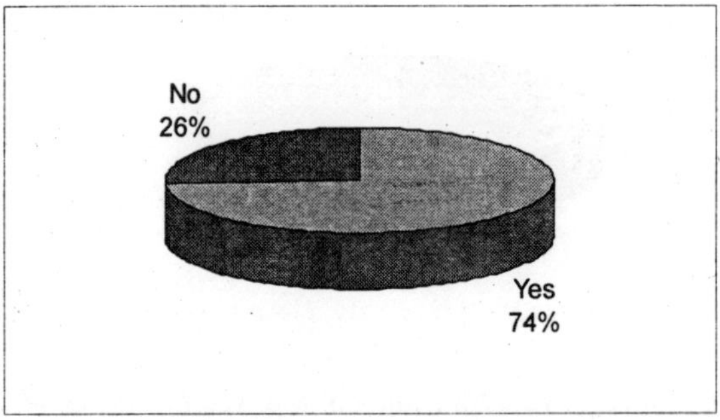

Fig. 35: Percentage Distribution on State Sports Federation of Manipur works very efficiently.

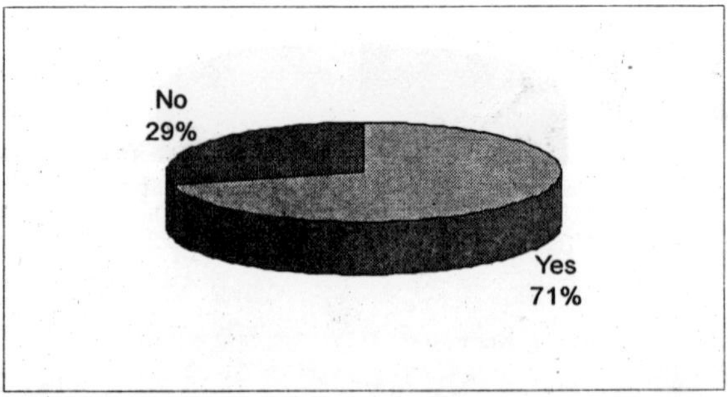

Fig. 36: Percentage Distribution on the Success of Manipuri women are only due to support of Federation.

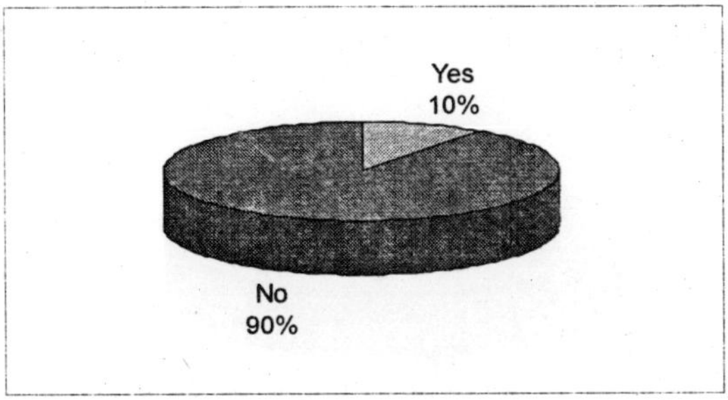

Fig. 37: Percentage Distribution on State Sports Federation are corrupt, and inefficient have done making for women sports.

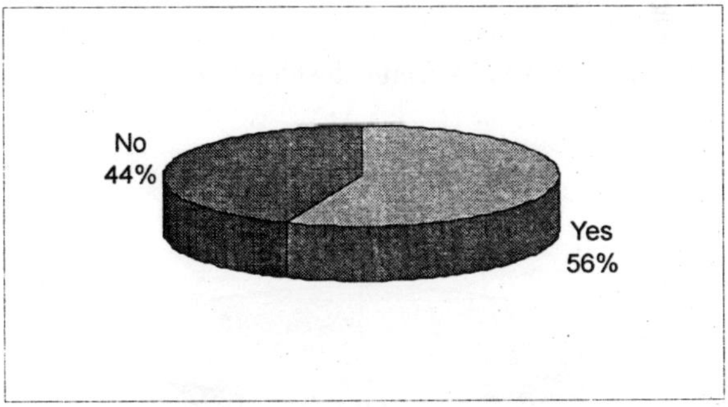

Fig. 38: Percentage Distribution on State Government have very strong sport policy to support women player.

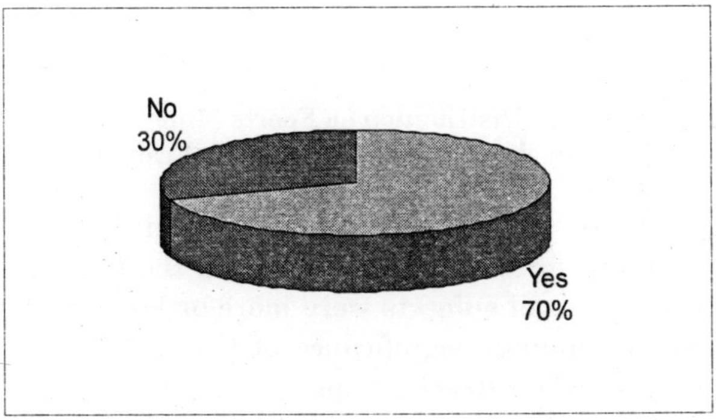

Fig. 39: Percentage Distribution on Political Environment is supportive for development of sports.

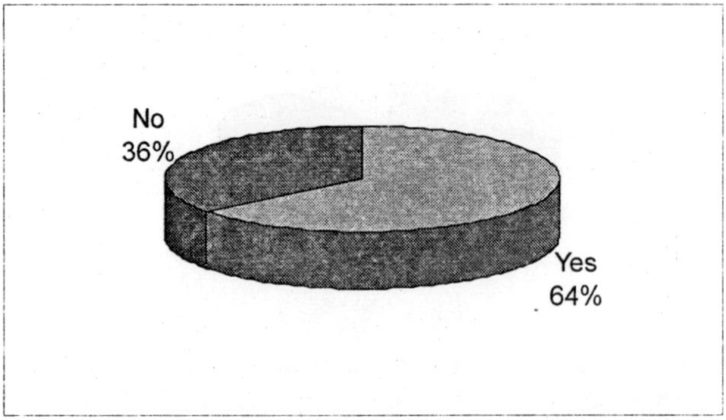

Fig. 40: Percentage Distribution on insurgency related situation and environment have affected development of sports in Manipur.

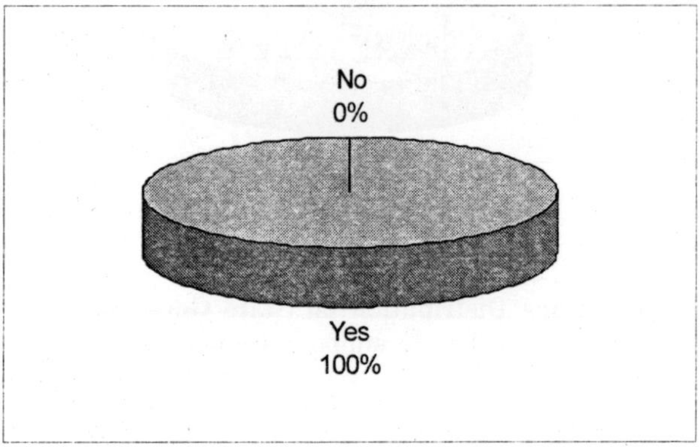

Fig. 41: Percentage Distribution on Sports Ministry is considered an important department in Ministerial cabinet.

Chi-square and percent analysis significantly revealed almost similar form of opinion and even the trend of opinion of five categories of subjects were more or less similar. Based on trends of opinion, significance of Chi-square it was seen invariably. All the subject groups are of opinion that Manipuri women participation in sports is mainly due to strong supportive social environment. With the social supportive environment the specific factors which contributed toward ultimately congenial environment were as follows:

- In Manipuri society women had equal status as men counterpart.
- Parents and society in fact is of supportive of women participating in sports. They did not consider this as against any tradition. Rather took it as means of development and scope for career.
- As a community also Manipuri society have a tradition of sports loving, enjoying and cultural heritage of celebrating festivating with sports.
- The folklore of heroic Manipuri women also served as ideal motivation factors as well as non-discrimination between women and male shall acceptance of equality of sex.
- Sportswomen achiever's popularity and celebrities status have become ideal to be followed by younger Manipuri women.
- It also added creation of conducive social environment for women sports.

Above are the prominent facts on which affirmative opinions of five subjects groups were overwhelmingly observed. These findings in term of observations clearly justifies, congenial sport supportive environment of Manipur for explosion for women sports.

In history of Manipur and Manipuri society above characteristic tradition and practices like equality of women status cultural heritage of sports in different form are well depicted.

Further opinion in areas of training scopes, facilities, career scopes, Government sports policy, the five categories of subject have opined affirmatively to different facts and reasons.

Opinion on these areas were assessed through questionnaires items. The statistical analysis showed all the five subject groups significantly opined that, employment scope and career opportunity that is available for sports women is one of the primary factors for popularity of sports among Manipuri women. In addition to these favourable physical structure and training scopes under various Government schemes and Sports Authority of India (SAI) have made plenty of opportunity of training and in realizing career and employment in sports.

The successful performance of Manipuri women at National and International level and successfully settling down in sports career has served as strong motive for Manipuri women to take up sports.

It is also seen, sponsorship is in form of employment and support from big Govt. and Non-Government agencies like Railways, CRPF, Indian Airlines, Local Clubs etc. have helped Manipuri Sportsman and women tremendously. Support from such sponsor is considered significantly better than the State Government organization in terms of employment of sports in Manipur. All such observations reflect clearly and honestly the existing scenario of sportswomen environment in Manipur. The role of sponsors like Railways, CRPF, Indian Airlines, Local Clubs etc. as measured employment and training opportunities provider can be seen very well from the number of recruit in this sponsors. CRPF, CISF, Railways and Soccer clubs of Goa are also major employer and sponsors.

Manipuri women have been dominating National sports scenario since at a decade. And successful performer have been employed all around India. The scenario has added to Manipuri women significantly preferring sports career as any other profession.

The infrastructure developed by State Government and Sports Authority of India provided training opportunity and facility. These have helped developing a kind of mass talent based in Manipur.

The significant facts that was also revealed from this survey study was that Manipuri Sports Organization and State Government Sports department are functioning efficiently as far opinions of women players, former players, Association Office Bearers of Sports, Sports Journalists, Coaches and SAI Office Bearers. Further Manipur is continuously affected by insurgency. But no insurgent groups has opposed functioning of sports organizations, policies etc. Rather sports have been encouraged by every section of society including the insurgents.

Hence all above findings clearly justify that the explosion of women sports in Manipur is because of most conducive and supportive cultural heritage, political and social environment, sports policy, employment scopes and above all people's characteristic as sports lovers.

5

Conclusion

Sports is the heart of any society. It serves to improve life and the social order. Today more nation compete in the Olympic Games than the number of nations affiliated to the United Nations. Throughout the world sports has a popular appeal among people of all ages and both sexes.

The women sports start with conditions as they are, and moves forward goals. The changing role of women in society from the Victorian age to the present manifests an enormous social revolution, in which sports have played a major role and thus the development of women sports in the present century definitely is one of the most fascinating topic.

There are myths related to females physical and psychological, masculination, the female's monthly cycles, pregnancy, the females physical and psychological limits of performance capacity. Most of this belief are rooted in long sociocultural attitudes. So, there are nations which actively oppose any competitive efforts from women.

In the past few decades, women sports have gained tremendous popularity all over globe. In India as well women sports is growing. In early days Indian women were discouraged to participate in sports. But today Indian women have earned more glory than their counterparts (men) in field of sports.

Manipur state is a very small state, but Manipur is one of the most popular state in India in games and sports. Though this state is still underdeveloped states in India, but the large number of sportswomen is very high in National and International level are from this state.

So, on the basis the present sports scenario of Manipur and the present researcher's experience and knowledge, it was intended to find out the cause of popularity of women sports in Manipur. Therefore the author, undertook the present study.

The purpose of the study was to find out the reasons or causes of explosion of women sports in Manipur.

For the purpose of the present study the research scholar investigated selected women players which have represented India or won laurel at National level in football, hockey, boxing, weight lifting, judo, cycling, fencing, teak-won-do and athletics. The other subjects involved in the present study were Ex-player, Office Bearers of Sports Association, Sports Journalists and Coaches and SAI Office Bearers. A total of 370 subjects were used as subjects for the purpose of the study.

The questionnaire method was used, and study of literature to collect relevant information for the purpose of the study. Questionnaire method was used to all subjects with 41 statements. All the statements were objective type of questionnaire with "Yes" and "No" options.

For the purpose of the present study the following aspects were selected for the preparation of questionnaire:

(a) Social Support

(b) Opportunity and Incentive Support

(c) Organization Functions & Sports Policy.

Total 380 questionnaires were administered through personal contact and mail but only 370 responded. The responses were categorized according to purpose of the study and results were drawn in term of descriptive technique of percentage and Chi-Square with .05 level of significance of each statement.

After the analysis by using descriptive technique of

percentage and Chi-Square. The reason or causes of explosion of women sports in Manipur was socially and traditionally encouraged for women participation in sports to participate the games, well supported from parents and associations, regularly organize the competition, available better employment scope, equal status with their counterpart (men), Women had take advantage of anatomical structure in games and sportswomen had availed standard sports facilities.

It was also revealed that, it required to improve the standard infrastructure, more budget for sport, training must be systematic. The functioning of association to be more effective. In college and school physical activity and physical education should be kept as compulsory subjects.

Conclusion

Within the limitation of present study the following conclusions may be drawn:

1) Social status of successful sportswomen encourage Manipuri women seriously take up games and sports.
2) In Manipur tradition and social environment is highly supportive for women sports.
3) Parents also encourage their daughter to participate the sports, and parents also provide every form of support required for sports participation and training.
4) Manipuri folklore of heroic women also serve as an ideal motivating factor to take sports.
5) Manipuri women has equal status to their counterpart men.
6) In Manipur there exists no social discrimination against women.
7) Structure and physical feature of manipuri women are suitable for sports.
8) The Manipuri women have to take up sports for job security and secure career. And also the prospect of getting

job is one of the main reasons to participate in sports.

9) Manipuri society have also culture and tradition of sports participation.

10) Women have more success in sports than male sports person and Manipuri women have dominating Indian women sports.

11) The success of Manipuri women at National and International arena has encouraged other Manipuri women to take up sports. Manipuri sportswomen like N. Kunjarani Devi is role model for other Manipuri women.

12) If given an opportunity Manipuri women would prefer other profession over sports.

13) In rural area as well women sports is very popular.

14) Social recognition is also a very strong factor for Manipuri women opting sports.

15) Manipuri women have participated in sports for sports scholarship, financial support etc. from govt.

16) The availability of standard sports facility have encouraged Manipuri women to take up sports.

17) SAI have contributed good number of sports facilities for Manipuri women played.

18) In Manipur compulsory Physical Education programme in school and college have made significant contribution in developing sports in women.

19) Central Government agencies like SAI's sports schemes have contributing in sports talent development.

20) All Games Associations have affiliated to the Federation.

21) In the State Sports Association there are very few political leaders involved. And players are not much satisfied for functioning of sports body.

22) In Manipur Sports Ministry was considered a important department in Ministerial cabinet.

Recommendations

In light of the above-mentioned conclusions drawn, on the basis of extensive research done on explosion of women sports in Manipur, the following recommendations are given:

1) It is recommended that the tradition and environment should be highly supportive for women sports.
2) It is recommended that the status of equal right and dignity should be kept on between male and female.
3) It is recommended that the Manipuri women should be given more job opportunity.
4) It is recommended that in rural area as well, sports should be promoted.
5) It is recommended that the availability of standard sports facilities should be promoted to encourage Manipuri women to take up sports.
6) It is recommended that SAI should promote more facilities for training.
7) It is recommended that in the schools physical education and sports should be kept as compulsory subject. And further there should be opportunity for training for all students at grass-root level.
8) It is recommended that the state sports department should regularly conduct sports meet and the maximum number of teams should be sent for National competition.
9) It is recommended that the political leaders should be not be encouraged to involve in Sports Associations.
10) It is recommended that the Associations should act properly for satisfaction of the players.

Appendices

APPENDIX - 1

Date: ....

To,

....

....

Dear Sir/Madam,

I am a Research Scholar with the Lakshmibai National Institute of Physical Education, Gwalior (M.P.), India. I have undertakes Doctoral Research entitled, "Explosion of women sports in Manipur – An Analytical Survey".

I shall be grateful if you would please spare a few minutes of your valuable time and complete the enclosed questionnaire. Your kind cooperation and valuable contribution will immensely enrich my study. And your response will be strictly kept confidential and only be used for research purpose.

I am enclosing herewith a self-addressed and stamped envelope for mailing the fill in questionnaire at your earliest convenience.

Thanking You.

Yours Truly,

(Y. Shantikumar Singh)

Enclosure: 1) Brief purpose of study

2) Questionnaire

3) Self Address and stamped envelop

APPENDIX – 2

Statement on Explosion of Women's Sports in Manipur

Name: .... Age..............

Address: ....

Date:..............

Designation: ....Education Status......................

1. Social status of successful sports women encourage Manipuri women's seriously take up games and sports. (Yes/No)
2. Manipuri Tradition and social environment is highly supportive for women sports. (Yes/No)
3. Manipuri parents encourage their daughter to participate sports. (Yes/No)
4. Manipuri folklore of heroic women also serves as an ideal motivating factor to take sports by Manipuri women. (Yes/No)
5. Manipuri women have equal right and dignified status like their men counterpart. (Yes/No)
6. There is no form of any social distimination excess against in Manipuri society. (Yes/No)
7. Parents provide every form of support required for sports participation and training. (Yes/No)
8. Structured and physical features of Manipuri women are suitable for sports. (Yes/No)
9. For Manipuri women sports offer a secure career. (Yes/No)
10. Manipuri women take up sports for job security. (Yes/No)
11. Manipuri societies have culture and tradition of sports participation. (Yes/No)

12. In state of Manipur sports provide better employment scope. (Yes/No)
13. Manipuri sportswomen are more successful than their counterpart man sports men. (Yes/No)
14. Manipuri sports women are dominating Indian women sports. (Yes/No)
15. The success of Manipuri women at National and International have encouraged other Manipuri women to take up sports. (Yes/No)
16. Sports women like N. Kunjarani Devi are idol for Manipuri women. (Yes/No)
17. Given a opportunity Manipuri women will prefer other profession over sports. (Yes/No)
18. Sports is not popular among rural women. (Yes/No)
19. Social recognition is one of the reason for Manipuri women opting sports. (Yes/No)
20. The prospect of getting job is main reason to participate in sports. (Yes/No)
21. Manipuri women participate in sports for sports scholarship, financial support etc. from govt. (Yes/No)
22. Availability of standard sports facility encourage Manipuri women to take up sports. (Yes/No)
23. SAI also have created good no. of sports facility.(Yes/No)
24. Compulsory Physical Education Programme in School and College have made significant contribution toward sports talent development at grass root level. (Yes/No)
25. Availability of sponsorship from National clubs etc. for better sports career and financial security for champions have greatly influenced Manipuri women. (Yes/No)
26. Central Government Agencies, like SAI's sports schemes have contributed in sports talent development. (Yes/No)

27. Is politics in Sports Organisation have helped in effective functioning of Sports Organisation? (Yes/No)
28. Are you satisfied with functioning of state sports body? (Yes/No)
29. Are all games associations affiliated to National Federation? (Yes/No)
30. A State Sports Associations used by Politicians for political purpose. (Yes/No)
31. State Sports department regularly conducted inter-school sports competition. (Yes/No)
32. Do you feel very few teams are sent to inter-university sports meet? (Yes/No)
33. Is more importance given to women sports for Manipuri Women's achieved records. (Yes/No)
34. State Sports Federation have played significant role in supporting women sports. (Yes/No)
35. State Sports Federation of Manipur works very efficiently. (Yes/No)
36. The success of Manipuri Women are only due to support of Federation. (Yes/No)
37. State Sports Federation are corrupt, and inefficient have done making for women sports. (Yes/No)
38. State Governments have very strong sport policy to support women player. (Yes/No)
39. Is Political Environment is supportive for development of sports. (Yes/No)
40. Is insurgency related situation and environment have affected development of sports in Manipur. (Yes/No)
41. Is sports Ministry considered an important department in Ministerial cabinet. (Yes/No)

APPENDIX - 3

Score of the responses on the explosion of the women's sports in Manipur

S.No.	Women Players		Ex-Players		Office Bearer Association of Sports		Sports Journalist		Coaches and SAI Office Bearers	
	Yes	No	Yes	No	Yes	No	Yes	No	Yes	No
1.	94	6	80	20	40	10	18	2	93	7
2.	88	22	72	28	36	14	14	6	69	31
3.	89	11	85	15	41	9	20	0	96	4
4.	86	14	72	28	50	0	18	2	89	11
5.	100	0	100	0	50	0	20	0	100	0
6.	68	32	59	41	29	21	19	1	80	20
7.	94	6	97	3	43	7	18	2	95	5
8.	93	7	91	9	49	1	20	0	81	19
9.	73	27	67	33	33	17	20	0	80	20
10.	54	46	59	41	25	25	8	12	59	41
11.	88	12	72	28	36	14	14	6	69	31
12.	69	36	68	32	32	18	17	3	82	18
13.	91	9	86	14	44	6	18	2	89	11
14.	71	29	60	40	47	3	14	6	87	13
15.	100	0	100	0	50	0	20	0	100	0
16.	100	0	100	0	50	0	20	0	100	0
17.	62	38	79	21	37	13	16	4	82	18
18.	37	63	49	51	26	24	9	11	41	59
19.	64	36	70	30	28	22	15	5	80	20
20.	64	36	68	32	32	18	17	3	82	18
21.	73	27	91	9	50	0	19	1	83	17
22.	66	34	74	26	37	13	18	2	68	32
23.	65	35	79	21	35	12	12	8	83	17
24.	67	33	77	23	50	0	10	10	67	33

(contd...)

25.	34	66	40	60	28	22	11	9	45	55
26.	77	23	72	28	39	11	16	4	87	13
27.	66	34	74	26	37	13	18	2	68	32
28.	31	69	70	30	50	0	10	10	58	42
29.	100	0	100	0	50	0	20	0	100	0
30.	8	92	12	88	3	47	1	19	16	84
31.	64	36	64	36	48	2	13	7	90	10
32.	54	46	65	35	38	12	14	6	74	26
33.	54	46	59	41	25	25	8	12	59	41
34.	67	33	77	23	50	0	10	10	67	33
35.	64	36	68	32	42	8	17	3	82	18
36.	48	52	65	35	47	3	18	2	84	16
37.	8	92	12	88	0	50	1	19	16	84
38.	51	49	49	51	48	2	2	18	58	42
39.	59	41	66	34	44	6	16	4	74	26
40.	62	38	71	29	34	16	12	8	66	44
41.	100	0	100	0	5	0	20	0	100	0

Bibliography

Books

All India council of sports, *Draft National Sports Policy* (New Delhi: Ministry of Education and Culture, 1980)

Bornns J., Hebbelink M. and Vernerando A., *"Women and Sports"* (S.Kargar Graphische Btriebe Coop Scheweiz. Basel 1981).

Boutılier A. Marry and Giovavanni Lucinda San, *The Sport Women* (Champaign Human Kinetics Publish,1983).

Cheska A.T., *Women's Sports-The Unlikely myth of Equality, A Socio-Pschyologicalsnd Kinanthropometric Approach* (Basel S. Karger 1981).

Eyler A.A. et.al, "Physical Activity and women in the United States: An overview of Health Benefits, Prevalence, and Intervention Opportunities,", *Women and Health* 26 (1997).

Henderson K.A. and Baileshki M.D., "Negotiating constraints to Women's Physical Recreation," *Society and Leisure* 16:2 (Fall 1993).

Kamlesh L. M. and Sangral M.S., *Principle and History of Physical Education* (Ludhiana: Prakash Brother,1981).

Kamlesh M.L.Dr., *Methodology of Research in Physical Education and Sports*, (Metropolitan Book Pvt. Ltd) 1986.

Larson, *Foundation of Physical Activity.*

Lever J., *"Sex Difference in Games children Play,"* Social Problems 24:3 (1976): 478- 487 cited by Bryanth J. Cratty, Psychology in contemporary Sports: Guideline for coaches and Athletes second edition (Englewood Cliffs, N.J. Prentice Hall Inc. 1983).

Lords Erik, "Increased Sports Opportunities for Women" *(the Chronicle of Higher Education)*.

Macmillan English Dictionary, (Macmillan Publisher's Limited) 2006.

Manorama Year Book 2006 (Malayala Manorama).

Martina Horner, "Fail: Bright Women," *Psychology Today* 3(1969).

Oxford English Dictionary (Paper book Encyclopedia Entries, London).

Singh Karan, "Study of Games and Sports Performance (men) of University of India Base on Inter- University Tournament Result of the Year (1981-82)" *University Sports* 5 (Sept;1982).

Singh M.K., *Women and Sports* (Jaipur: Rawat Publication, 1990).

Singh Nisha, *Women Education*; Women University News38 (February 14, 2000)

Thomas J.R. and Nelson J.K., *"Research Method in Physical Activity"* (Human Kinetic, Publication 2001).

Uppal K.A., *Foundation of Physical Education* (Delhi: Friends Publication, 1994)

Ayers Barara, "A study of Parental Attitude toward value of Physical Education in Total Development of the Daughter" *Completed Research in Health, Physical Education and Recreation* 6(1964).

Ballmann L. Katie, The Development of the Physical Activity Acceptance Scale: Determining Gender views on Female Participation in Traditionally Musculine Sports and Exercise Activity," *Research Quarterly for Exercise and Sports* 68(March 1997 Supplement).

Barbara J.R, "Attitude of High School Girls and Their Parents toward Physical Education," *Completed Research in Health, Physical Education* 12 (1970).

Barnett N.P. and Wright P., Psychological consideration for Women and Sports," Clinic in Sports Medicine 13:2 (April 1994): 207-313 cited in *Sports Documentation Monthly Bulletin* 24:5 (May 1994).

Broer Marion R., Fox Katharine S. and Way Eunice, "Attitude of University of Washington Women Student Toward Physical Education and Activity," *Research Quarterly* 26 (Dec. 1955).

Cash T.F. et. al, "Why do Women Exercise? Factor Analysis and Further Validation of the Reason for Exercise Inventory", Perceptual and motor skill 78.2 (April1994): 539-544 cited in Sports *Documentation Monthly Bulletin* 24:4 (April 1994).

Chapman Nancy L., "An Investigation of the prediction of success in Women's Field Hockey," *Dissertation Abstracts International,* 1947.

Ebbeck Vicki et.al, "Reasons for Adult Participation in Physical Activity : An Internal Approach," *International Journal of Sports Psychology* 26(1995).

Elder J.P. et al., "Direct Home Observation of the Promoting of Physical Activity in Sedentary and Active Mexican and Anglo-American children," *Journal of Development and Behavioral Pediatrics* 19(1998).

Flores Alfredo José *et al., "Women's sports coverage still lacking"* (The American Society of Newspaper Editors).

Gill K. and Overdorf V., "Incentives for Exercise in younger and older Women," *Journal of Sports Behavior* 17;2(June 1994).

Grant Long, "Cohesion: A predictor of team Success," *Completed Research in Health Physical Education and Recreation,* 15 (1973);126

Greendorfer S. and Lewko J., "Role of Family members in sport Socialization of Children," *Research Quarterly* 49(1978).

Isenberger Wilma, "Self Attitude of Women Physical Education Major Students and of women physical education teacher," *Research Quarterly* 30(march 1959).

Kapper Eneline E., " Inventory to Determine of College women Toward Physical Education and Students service of Physical Education Department," *Research Quarterly* (march 1953).

Kaushika Priyanka, "*Give them a Sporting chance*" (Education Times).

Keeneth R. Fox, Charlos B. Corbin and William H. Couldry, "Female Physical Estimation and Attraction to Physical Activity," *Journal of sports Psychology* 7 (June 1985).

Kumar Rajiv, *Village Girls bend it like Beckham* (times of India).

Lenney E., "*Women's self confidence in achievement Situation,*" Psychology Bulletin 84(1977).

Martin Curtis Eugene, "Analysis of the Attitude of Elementary School Teacher and Administrator Toward Athletic for Female" *Dissertation Abstract International* (Oct. 1979).

Masse L.C. et. at., "Physical Activity in Midlife, Older, and Minority Women: Issues from an Expert Penal," *Journal of Women's Health 7* (1998).

Morse Leslie, "*American Athlete Moves One Step Closer to Her Dream of 2004 Olympics*" Google Search (internet)

Nugent, "Preadolescent Females" Preference and Attitudes toward outside School Physical Activities during a 2 year intervention", *Research Quarterly for Exercise and sports* 68 (March 1997 supplement).

Ogynjivenjo Ogunbiyi Daniel, "the Development of Nigeria's Participation in International Sports competition and its effect on the National", *Dissertation abstracts International* 39 (February 1978).

Raugh Dorothy and Wall Robert, "Measuring sports Participation," *International Journal of Sports Psychology* 18(1987):112

Report of the all India survey on college and Institution of Physical Education, Educational Survey NCERT, New Delhi, 1967.

Rowe D. and Brown A., "Promoting Women's Sports: Theory, Policy and practice," Leisure Studies (GBR): 3 Cited in *Sports Documentation Monthly Bulletin* 24 (January 1994).

Ryckman Ricard M. and Hamel Jane, "Female Adolescents Motives Related to involvement in organized team Sport" *International journal of Sports Psychology* 23 (April-June) 1992.

Saxena Siddharth, *The Sun always Shines on Manipur, Sunday Times of India,* 2007,5th Feb. New Delhi).

Silva John M. and Andrew J. Albert, "An Anlysis of game location and Basketball Performance in the Atlantic coast Conference," *International Journal of Sport Psychology* 18(1987).

Singh Balbir, "Disasters of Today," *The Hindustan Times* Sunday Magazine.

Smith Y.R., " Women of color in society and sports," Quest (USA) 44 (August 1992) : 228-250 cited in *Sports Documentation, Monthly Bulletin* 22.

Snyder E. and Kivlin J., "Women Athletes and Aspects of Psychological well-being and Body Image," *Research Quarterly* 46(1975).

Suggs Welch, "Most Americans Favor Cutting Men's Sports to Add Women's, Poll Finds", *Chronicle of Higher Education Bulletin.*

Thapar K.D., "Right Attitude Imperative for success in sports," *SNIPS Journal* (April 1981)

Zeelei M.Potgieter, "Perception of Female sports Participation," *SA Journal for Research in Sports, Physical Education and Recreation* 14(1991): 77-82 cited in *Sports Documentation Monthly Bulletin* 23 January 1993.

Unpublished Theses

Bajwa, Kamwaljit Sing, "An Analysis of the Causes of Failure of Indian Basketball Team in the Asia Competition," Unpublished M.P.E. Thesis, Punjabi Unversity, Patiala, 1974.

Kaur, Sukhdeep, "Causes of poor Performance of Indian Hockey *at International level and its remedies"* Unpublished MPE Thesis Jiwaji University, Gwalior, 1987.

Index

■ ■ ■